WB   27. 11 87

THE ARTHUR NEGUS GUIDE TO
BRITISH GLASS

The Arthur Negus
Guide to British

GLASS

JOHN BROOKS

Foreword by Arthur Negus

Consultant Editor: Arthur Negus

Hamlyn

London · New York · Sydney · Toronto

Frontispiece: Goblet on a cut glass stem, *c.* 1740. It has been wheel-engraved with the motto of the Walpoles (*'Fari quae Sentio'*) and 'Prosperity to Houghton'. Museum of London.

Published by
The Hamlyn Publishing Group Limited
London · New York · Sydney · Toronto
Astronaut House
Feltham, Middlesex
England

© Copyright J. A. Brooks 1981

ISBN 0 600 34218 2

Printed in Italy

Acknowledgements

All the photographs in this book were provided by the author with the exception of the following:
British Museum, London 3, 13; Cooper-Bridgeman Library, London 132; Fitzwilliam Museum, Cambridge 6, 10; Hamlyn Group – Thomas Photos 19, 20, 22, 92, 94, 107, 108, 109, 111, 122, 123, 124, 127, 128, 129, 130, 131, 133, 134, 142, 143; Hamlyn Group Picture Library 21, 135, 144, 145; Museum of London 9, 58; National Portrait Gallery, London 11, 12; Pilkington Glass Museum, St Helens 14, 34, 40, 101, 125; Science Museum, London 4, 5; Sotheby Parke Bernet & Co, London 7, 8, 24, 35, 66, 67, 68, 91, 93, 110, 113, 114, 115, 116; Victoria and Albert Museum, London 90, 102, 104.
The line drawings are by The Hayward Art Group.

Contents

Foreword by Arthur Negus

Several years ago it was possible to buy eighteenth-century English wine glasses for a few pounds each—although practically every other section of the Fine Arts had increased considerably in value, glass seemed to be left behind. Today the situation has changed, an increasing number of people are beginning to collect glass, attracted by both its beauty and its elegance. Eighteenth-century wine glasses are now more costly because of this, but an interesting collection of glassware may still be amassed by the discerning collector who is prepared to devote some time and effort.

The author of this book, John Brooks, may frequently be seen at Antiques Fairs throughout the country. He is that happy combination of expert and enthusiast, and in passing on some of his expertise to the reader I feel that he has also conveyed some of his own enjoyment. Much good information is given in these pages, and (with the exception of some early rarities) the illustrations are confined to glassware that is in the hands of private collectors, to demonstrate the opportunities that are still open to collectors. I have no hesitation in recommending this work as a worthwhile addition to this series of reference books.

Arthur Negus

Author's note

The story of the development of the glass industry falls into two distinct periods, the first up to 1700, before which time so few examples of glassware survive that one's interest must be largely academic. It is, however, necessary to have some knowledge of the development of the trade to set the scene for the period after 1700 when the manufacture of domestic glass increased to such an extent that many thousands of examples survive today in museums and private collections. This is the period of interest to collectors, and what I have to say is based upon proven fact and commonly accepted opinion. But twenty years of interest in the subject has led me to a number of opinions and conclusions of my own which I find other authors have not discussed. In addition, after years of talking to collectors of all degrees of experience, I have found that there are certain questions or problems which arise time and time again. I have tried to deal with these in a way which I hope will be of value to anyone to whom this is a new interest.

I have given a reading list at the end of the text and tried to point out what I feel to be the particular value of each book. Where my narrative is brief and lacks detail these books will compensate for my shortcomings.

This book, then, is intended to appeal to several groups of readers. To the person who was unaware that there was any history in the development of glassmaking in the British Isles in the hope that it will reveal in some degree what an ordinary domestic article can tell us about our past. To the budding collector whose enthusiasm has been recently acquired, in the hope that it will both inform and stimulate him or her to further interest and reading on the subject. To the experienced and knowledgeable collector, in the hope that my own opinions will either confirm your own conclusions, give you cause for further reflection, or where you disagree strongly, to stimulate further research and discussion on the subject.

Chapter 1

Glass: Its nature
and early history

For many centuries glass has been an important material to developing societies, to such an extent that I doubt whether our modern technological world could function without it. In our own domestic lives I am sure that we all take the many uses of glass entirely for granted, but pause to reflect how different our lives would be without it. No windows, no television, no light bulbs, and although one can drink from a variety of other vessels I imagine there are very few homes which don't boast a set of good drinking glasses to grace the dinner table. It is a material which satisfies both functional and aesthetic needs.

To appreciate the true romance of the development of the glass industry which the following pages catalogue, I would like you to try and forget that it is the commonplace material of today and imagine instead that glass is a rarity and glassmaking is an art surrounded in mystery and practised for the benefit of a privileged few; to provide windows for the larger churches and drinking vessels for the rich and powerful.

Glass does occur naturally in some parts of the world, as a result of volcanic action to form a material usually called obsidian, and as rock crystal, a particularly clear form of quartz. Both these materials have been used to produce decorative and ritual objects, but there has never been enough for widespread use, and they can only be worked upon by laborious methods such as carving and grinding. Imagine, therefore, the impact of a process which can produce from the most unlikely materials (sand and wood ash) an endless supply of a substitute for these rare and desirable natural minerals that can be wrought easily into shapes which previously took endless time and trouble to produce from a solid lump of material.

Today the concept of a solid material which is completely transparent does not trouble us at all, but when clear glass was first produced long before the beginning of the Christian era the whole idea of being able to see something which one could not reach because of a near invisible barrier would have seemed akin to magic. One has only to watch a fly buzzing at a window, able to see daylight but unable to understand the impediment to its progress, to see what I mean. The whole history of glassmaking until recent times has been surrounded by this air of mystery and secrecy which I am sure the glassmakers did their best to promote, since it enabled them to keep firm control over the industry and limit the spread of knowledge of the art to those whom they chose.

For instance, Assyrian clay tablets of the seventh century B.C. bear inscriptions giving recipes for glass which stress the necessity to placate the spirits and observe the true ceremony required to produce a satisfactory product.

When Venice was at the height of its importance as a glassmaking centre (the fifteenth to seventeenth centuries A.D.) laws were passed to prohibit any Venetian glassmaker practising his craft anywhere other than Murano. In an article of the Statutes of 1454 it was ordered that if any workman of any kind should transport his craft into a foreign country and refuse to return an emissary should be commissioned to slay him. There is evidence that this threat was carried out several times. In letters patent of September 1567 John le Carré was given a licence to make glass in England for a period of twenty-one years. One of the conditions was that the French glass makers he proposed to import to carry out the work should teach and train Englishmen. In the event his Lorraine glass makers, rather than do this, quit their jobs and returned to France. These recorded instances indicate how closely the glassmakers guarded their art and how mysterious a process it must have seemed to the general public.

How glass is made

I have already mentioned the materials used to make glass and before starting on the history of the development of glass making in England and Ireland it may be appropriate to consider both the material itself and the basic techniques used to fashion it.

Basically glass is made from one of the various forms of silica: sand, quartz, flint. The temperatures required to melt these on their own are so high as to be uneconomical and the resultant glass is too viscous for practical use. However, with the addition of a flux this temperature is reduced by about half and glassmaking becomes possible. How this technique was first discovered no-one knows, although evidence of glassmaking goes back some 3500 years. The two principal fluxes which have traditionally been used are carbonate of potash and carbonate of soda. The former was generally obtained from the ashes of burnt vegetation, i.e. brushwood, branches and leaves, while the latter came from natural mineral deposits (Pliny refers to deposits imported from Lower Egypt) or the ashes of a marine plant called Barrilla obtained from Spain. As a general rule potash-based glass was a product of Northern Europe where forests were abundant, the glass produced having a marked green tint. Soda-based glass was a Mediterranean product which in the hands of the Venetian glass makers became a fine clear glass they termed 'cristallo'.

The other important additions to glass were lime, which helped to produce a harder and whiter metal, and lead oxide which produced the English 'lead crystal' glass with which much of our story will be concerned. In more recent times other elements such as barium, strontium and titanium, have been added to produce glass for special purposes.

In spite of the secrecy surrounding the art of glassmaking, written records trace its history as far back as the Assyrian tablets already noted. Pictorial evidence certainly goes back as far as an eleventh century manuscript which shows the various basic operations of glassmaking in progress. Remarkably, the method of making glass by hand has changed little since the discovery of glass blowing in the first century B.C. Indeed,

1 An engraving from an eighteenth century encyclopedia showing the several stages in the manufacture of a drinking glass.

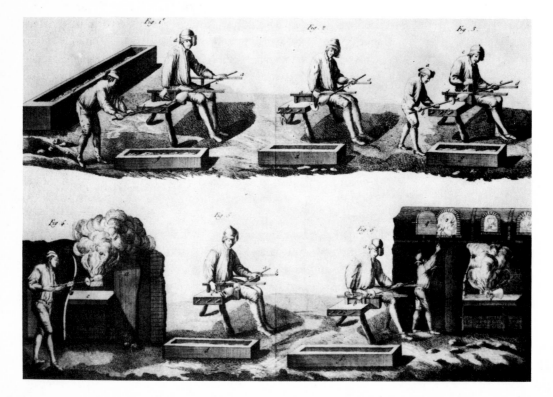

practically all the basic manufacturing and decorating techniques known today have been in existence for at least 2000 years; they include cutting, engraving, gilding, carved overlaid colours and the use of colour. The only important form of decoration to be developed since the beginning of the Christian era was the white lacy pattern invented by the Venetians in the sixteenth century and which English glassmakers revived as the opaque twist stem of wine glasses in the eighteenth century.

It is clear, then, that only the simplest tools are necessary – a metal tube on which to gather and blow the molten glass, pincers to stretch and draw it, shears to cut it and a holder to carry it when it is completed.

Hand made vessel glass is traditionally made by a team of three or four men called a chair. This takes its name from the chair or bench on which the leader of the team sits, and which has long arms extending in front of him. In the case of a drinking glass the leader, or gaffer, blows the glass bubble which will become the bowl, other members of the team apply the stem and foot to this bubble and then an iron bar termed the pontil iron, heated at one end, is applied to the under side of the foot. The bubble is then cut away from the blowing iron leaving the glass, with a bowl of irregular shape, supported on the pontil iron. The gaffer supports this across the arms of his chair and whilst rolling it back and forth with one hand, manipulates the bowl to the desired shape with a small forming tool of wood or metal held in the other. Since the glass only remains plastic within a particular temperature range it may be necessary to offer the glass up to the mouth of the furnace to reheat it several times during the course of manufacture. (People often comment on the fact that so many eighteenth century glasses have stems which are neither straight nor at right angles to the foot. With the foregoing in mind it will be obvious that with a hot, plastic glass held parallel to the floor there will be a tendency for it to droop, which is neutralised by the rolling along the arms of the chair. But at whatever point the gaffer stops it spinning, if it is still soft enough it will show some small tendency to bend out of square to the foot which is at right angles to the floor.)

The glass is then separated from the pontil iron and because the reheating process induces internal stresses in the glass it is transferred to a section of the oven where it can be annealed by reducing the temperature gradually.

I have yet to meet anyone who is not fascinated by the sight of a skilled glass blower at work, and even when one can see a

2 Three Roman bottles from the second century A.D. The one on the far right is pierced in imitation of a sea urchin.

glass vessel taking shape before one's eyes there is still that hint of magic and mystery about it that has always made glass a desirable material right down the centuries.

There is one other fact about glass which I may mention at this time and that is that it does not deteriorate with age. I have seen glassware made in Roman times looking as clear and as pristine as if it were made today. Indeed, this is one aspect of the material that concerns would-be collectors because if it doesn't change how can one tell the difference in two pieces of glass made several centuries apart. This is one of the things I hope to explain in this book.

Wealden glass

The earliest glass to have been discovered in Britain dates from Roman times. It is unclear whether this was made here or was imported; the majority of it is tied in style to the glass known to have been made in Northern Europe, particularly Germany. My own feeling is that with the difficulties of transport it could have been easier and more economical to set up furnaces in places where there was a demand. However, no proven glasshouse sites of this period have yet come to light and the problem cannot be resolved on the basis of style, since under Roman influence the same styles were made throughout the Roman Empire.

After the decline of Roman influence, regional styles did start to emerge but glassware of the post-Roman years found in this country still displays this general Northern European fashion.

It is not until the advent of written records that we have any further knowledge of the history of glassmaking. The Venerable Bede in his *Ecclesiastical History*, wrote that in A.D. 675, for his church and monastery in Wearmouth, Benedict Biscop 'sent messengers to Gaul to fetch makers of Glass who were unknown in Britain at this time, that they might glaze the windows of his church'. Again in 758 Cuthbert, Bishop of Jarrow, wrote to Lullus, Bishop of Mayence, 'If there be any man in your diocese who can make vessels of glass well, pray send him to me, I beg your fraternity that you will persuade him to come to us, for we are ignorant and helpless in that art.' These suggest that in the north of England, at least, the knowledge of glassmaking had disappeared.

I think that there is more likelihood that, whatever glass-making was undertaken in this country was done in the south of England in that area of Sussex and Surrey known as the Weald. The earliest records and evidence of an established and continuous glass industry all point to it having settled around the area of Chiddingfold in Surrey. From work carried out by the Reverend T. S. Cooper and S. E. Winbolt in the early years of this century, and more recently by G. H. Kenyon and Mrs. E. S. Godfrey we have built up a picture of an industry which operated somewhat precariously from the early years of the thirteenth century to the mid-sixteenth century and after the arrival of le Carré an expanding industry given a new lease of life as a result of a vastly improved product.

The first certain records of glassmaking establishing itself is with the grant of twenty acres of land in Chiddingfold to Laurence Vitrearius in 1226. He was probably a Norman glassmaker and after establishing himself he received contracts for the glazing of Westminster Abbey. Records point to his descendants continuing as glassmakers into the fourteenth century when another family, the Schurterres, make their appearance. Then in the fifteenth century the Peytowes make an appearance. Although all these families settled on the Weald and ultimately became good yeoman stock I feel that they were all originally immigrant craftsmen working in the French Lorraine and Norman traditions. At that time French glass-making was much more highly developed than ours. Most of their business was in window glass, which the French supplied for the glazing of all the great churches and abbeys which were being built during the thirteenth to fifteenth centuries.

Why they settled at Chiddingfold is uncertain because of the three essentials for glassmaking—fuel, sand and clay for pots—only fuel was present in abundance. This was the bulkiest of the three, and was needed in considerable quantities, both as fuel for the furnaces and to provide wood ash as the source of potash. If one had to transport anything into the area, clay in relatively small quantities and sand were the easiest to manage.

3 A beaker found at Kempston, Bedfordshire, dating from the late fifth century A.D. It is green with both horizontal and vertical trails. British Museum, London.

The glass furnaces themselves were generally small structures of about 12 ft. long by 6 ft. wide and 4 ft 6 in. high. There were openings along each side giving access to the glass pots which sat, probably two or four to a side, on shelves either side of the central furnace, which was fed from either end. The glass pots varied, but a typical size was about 12 inches diameter by 12 inches high, holding some two to three gallons of molten glass. These small furnaces could be built fairly quickly and, when sources of fuel in the immediate vicinity were exhausted, abandoned and new ones established close to fresh woodlands.

The product was principally window glass, made by both the crown and broad sheet methods, and the number of men employed at each furnace being from two to four. As the great period of ecclesiastical building continued the demand for stained glass increased, and all authorities are agreed that as this was an art not practised in this country, France became the new source of window glass, and demand for clear window glass diminished. Since few private owners could afford glazed windows the market was then only for replacements. The glassmakers of the Weald obviously didn't supply glass for the windows of all the great abbeys around the country. There is evidence of glasshouses at Salisbury and Rugeley in Staffordshire, but nowhere else has such a concentration of glasshouse sites been discovered as at Chiddingfold and nowhere else has evidence survived of continuous glassmaking over such a long period.

Vessel glass had always been a minor part of the business. The quality of the glass and the skill of the operatives did not lend itself to elaborate or sophisticated vessel glass. Most of the vessels they turned out appear to have been for medical or chemical uses. From earliest times the manufacture of urinals is recorded.

By the middle of the sixteenth century glassmaking in England seems almost to have disappeared. At the same time the Venetian glass trade based on Murano was becoming famous for the quality and style of its 'cristallo' wares and there was undoubtedly a growing market amongst the European nobility for these fine glass wares. As early as 1398 Venetian ships had been allowed into the port of London to sell glass and earthenware vessels. Henry VIII had his glassware mounted in gold.

Thus the arrival of John le Carré in London in 1567 signalled a new lease of life for the English glass trade.

Le Carré was a native of Arras in Northern France, which at that time was part of the Low Countries. A merchant with

4, 5 *Above and opposite:* Two stages in the manufacture of glass at an eighteenth century English glass furnace. *Above:* Glass is blown. *Opposite:* The glass is cast. These are engravings by Henri Gravelot, a French artist working in England 1733-45.

connections in the glass trade, he probably came to England, where Queen Elizabeth was on the throne, to escape religious persecution, since he was a Calvinist and Protestant, and also because he had a daughter who had married and settled in London.

Presumably he soon discovered the opportunities that existed to develop glassmaking, and in conjunction with several others, including his son-in-law, applied for and got licences to open a window glasshouse on the Weald and a furnace to make the Venetian style of glass in London. After further negotiations he was finally granted a monopoly for a term of twenty-one years. The actual terms of le Carré's patent were that:

1. Anyone infringing the patent was liable to have his tools, work and supplies confiscated and be required to pay £100.

2. The patentees had to produce sufficient glass to satisfy the home market.

3. The glass was to be as cheap or cheaper than imported glass.

4. They were to teach Englishmen the art of glassmaking so that at the expiry of the patent the trade would be in the hands of natives.

5. The patentees to pay the Crown at least as much as would have been raised by taxing imported glass, although the import of glass was not abandoned.

6. The patent was to lapse at Christmas 1568 if the licensees were not producing enough glass to satisfy domestic requirements.

With the granting of his monopoly le Carré contracted with Thomas and Balthazar Hennezell to come to England and bring four other 'gentlemen glass makers' with them. These included members of the Thisac and Thietry families, later to become famous in the history of English glassmaking as Tyzack and Tittery. These were glassmakers in the Lorraine tradition but le Carré also attracted Norman glassmakers named de Bangard (later Bungar) to make crown glass in the Weald glasshouse.

Trouble eventually arose over item four in the monopoly quoted above, when the Lorrainers refused point-blank to pass on their knowledge to English operatives. Rather than do this they returned to France. The Bungars also refused to fulfil this condition. This led to a Court enquiry which decided that there was no hope that the glassmakers would honour that part of the licence and that it should not be enforced, for it was in the best interests of the country that glassmaking should continue.

In 1570 le Carré introduced Venetian craftsmen into his London 'cristallo' glasshouse, and decided to concentrate his efforts on improving the Wealden vessel glass. However, he died in 1572 before making any great progress in that direction.

Glassmaking continued after the death of le Carré, but his partners were divided among themselves. Lawsuits were undertaken, taxes due under the monopoly were not paid, and other French glassmakers entered the country and set up in competition. By 1576 the patent had fallen into abeyance. This state of affairs brought to the fore the next important figure in our story, and the last man of any importance to make his mark on the history of glassmaking in this country before the advent of coal fired furnaces. The man was Jacob Verzelini, who was a Venetian glassmaker originally brought to London in 1570 by le Carré to make crystal glass in the Venetian style. He was born in Venice in 1522, moved to Antwerp in 1549 (presumably in defiance of the laws controlling glassmakers) and married there in 1556. After the death of le Carré, he appears to have taken over the glasshouse at the Crutched Friars.

By 1575 Verzelini was sufficiently well established to apply for, and obtain, a licence for a monopoly of fine crystal glassmaking in England. This was, strictly speaking, before the expiry of le Carré's patent, but as we have shown this was inoperative anyway. The one important condition he procured, which le Carré had not been able to do, was the ban on imports of foreign glass which might compete with his own product, and there are records showing that he took action when necessary to protect his patent.

6 An English glass goblet, dated 1578, from the glasshouse of Jacob Verzelini. Fitzwilliam Museum, Cambridge.

Glasses have survived which are attributed to Verzelini's glasshouse, or to his period. In this country they may be seen at the Victoria and Albert Museum, the British Museum and the Fitzwilliam Museum in Cambridge. These glasses are mostly engraved, and where dates appear they coincide with the period when Verzelini's glasshouse was working in Broad Street. The style is basically Venetian, but show variations which must be attributed to local requirements and preferences. Against all the odds another glass in this group turned up in a private house in England as recently as 1978. It was dated 1584, which meant it had led a charmed life for nearly 400 years. Are there any more to be found?

Verzelini became a respected and established figure in England and died in 1606 at the age of 84. He is buried with his wife at Downes Church in Kent, where they are commemorated by a pair of brasses.

After the death of Verzelini and the expiry of his patent in 1596 the whole glass trade was heading for a complete change of direction. The trade was about to become organised under the influence of Englishmen for the first time. The introduction of coal fired furnaces was instrumental in this change.

During the latter half of the sixteenth century glassmaking in the Wealden tradition had continued around Chiddingfold with a marked improvement in the quality of the wares they produced. This was undoubtedly due to the influx of new craftsmen brought into the country by le Carré. As these new glassmaking families increased they spread their influence westwards and northwards, opening up new sites in Staffordshire and Shropshire. Landowners encouraged them, since glassmaking created revenue by the sale of wood and Staffordshire produced a supply of clay ideally suited for glass pots.

Coal and Sir Robert Mansell

More and more industries were becoming the subject of monopolies during the reign of Elizabeth I, the monopolies being granted to courtiers and favourites as rewards for service. For the crown it was a cheap way of rewarding the recipients, since it cost the exchequer nothing. Indeed the crown profited from the levies which the monopolists had to pay for their privileges.

One man who obtained such a monopoly was Sir Jerome Bowes. With Verzelini's patent due to expire at the end of 1595 he was awarded a twelve-year monopoly in 1592 to take over when the other was ended, for a fixed levy of 100 marks per year. Bowes appears to have had some trouble in maintaining a supply of glass to the market, since Verzelini's sons continued in production at Broad Street. Eventually Bowes made an arrangement with two London businessmen, Turner and Robson, that they should take over glassmaking under the term of his monopoly in return for £500 per annum. After his payment to the Crown this left him with a profit without having to do anything for it himself. Turner and Robson, by dubious means, put the Verzelinis out of business, took over their staff and went into production at Blackfriars. Bowes had various problems over illegal imports and others trying to set up in competition, but armed with a new patent to run for a further twenty-one years, and as a result of actions through the courts, by 1610 he was in sole command of all crystal glassmaking in England, and the trade for the first time was in the hands of Englishmen, even though most of the work was still being carried out by Venetian craftsmen.

The increase in the glassmaking industry began to have serious repercussions on the woodlands of Britain. The Wealden glasshouses were consuming ever-increasing quantities of timber and numerous accounts record the denuding of large areas of woodland on the Sussex/Surrey borders. The land-owners often had more concern for the income from their timber than the preservation of their woodlands. By 1580 the demands of the glass and iron smelting industries made the situation critical and laws were passed controlling the erection of new iron furnaces, and in 1584 a Bill was introduced to limit the operation of glasshouses, requesting that all foreign craftsmen be prevented from operating at all, and that native Englishmen should not operate within thirty miles of London. These terms were somewhat modified in the event, but we may gather from this the concern that the problem was causing.

Transport, over such roads as existed at that time, was expensive and laborious. The glasshouses being small it was easier to move them when supplies of fuel close to hand were exhausted. This was not the case with the iron smelters. Their works, being bigger, were static and fuel had to be brought from as far as was necessary. This did not endear the glassmakers to the iron smelters, whose operation suggests to me that of locusts. The practice of coppicing, or the planned regeneration of the woodlands, either did not appear to have been known or was not widely developed.

The big problem, however, was that the further afield the glassmakers had to travel to establish themselves, the more problems they created regarding access to markets. Waterways were the favourite routes of communication for most manufac-tured products, and various Bills introduced into Parliament were aimed at pushing the consumers of wood further and further from these lines of communication.

With these pressures upon the industry, the advent of coal fired furnaces was in the long term to prove the salvation of the trade. But such was the conservatism of the glassmakers that the transition was not achieved easily or willingly.

The first record of a patent taken out to cover the use of coal in furnaces was in 1610. This was worded to cover all industrial processes requiring the use of a furnace, but in the following year another patent was granted which was aimed specifically at glassmaking. This patent was sought by Sir Edward Zouch, Bevis Thelwell and Thomas Percival with others. Percival is the person actually credited with the invention of the coal-fired furnace. Zouch then came into conflict with Robson (who had bought out the patent of Sir J. Bowes) over who should make what; and how, but the former, after successful lobbying of the Court, managed to obtain, in 1614, a new patent for twenty-one years, to cover the use of coal in glassmaking, which revoked all other patents, forbade the use of wood and banned importation of foreign-made products. Whereas the original patent regarding the use of coal was of the type we know today, protecting the method only, this last one was a monopoly patent which gave the most wide-ranging protection to its holders of any patent so far issued. They proceeded to bring pressure to bear on Robson, and eventually forced him out of business. They pursued similar courses with the forest glassmakers, and in 1615 secured themselves with yet another patent which included, for the first time, the name of Sir Robert Mansell.

This is the first we hear of Sir Robert, but for the next forty years, until his death in 1656, the glass trade was to revolve around him.

Before pursuing the thread of our story, let us pause to consider the question of coal fired furnaces. Although the declared aim of the patents regarding the use of coal was to relieve the pressure on the forests and woodlands of England, its protagonists must also have been aware that a new technology was required to make effective use of it.

Wood-burning furnaces used open-topped crucibles with the flames circulating freely around and over them. The fumes from coal used in the same manner contained carbon and sulphur, which discoloured the glass. This problem was solved by enclosing the tops of the glass pots, but then it was found that higher temperatures were required to melt the raw materials. This led to modifications in furnace design to increase the draught and the head generated.

Although the introduction of coal was resisted (in fact it would seem that nearly two hundred years were to pass before it was accepted in Europe) this patent was to prove to be one of the great turning points in the development of the English glass trade. Not only was it a step forward in the technology of glassmaking, but because it was protected by patent, the holders of the patent had the opportunity to dominate and control the progress and direction of glassmaking in this country.

The arrival of le Carré some sixty years earlier had revived what was an ailing and declining industry. The new impetus provided by the coal burning process allowed it to be organised in a manner which was to lead to the dominance of English glassmaking in the eighteenth century.

Since the new patent had such a fundamental effect on the operation of glassmaking, whoever controlled the patent was in a position to control the whole industry. The patents had been granted in several names: Zouch, Thelwell, Percival. While they undoubtedly perfected the process they were also involved in litigation over several years with Robson and the Wealden glassmakers over patent infringements. It was not until the appearance of one strong directing influence that the financial and economic opportunities offered by the patent could be exploited. This influence appeared in the person of Sir Robert Mansell.

Mansell was born in 1573, the eighth son of Sir Edward Mansell of Margam in Glamorgan. At the age of fifteen he served under Lord Howard against the Armada: he earned a knighthood at Cadiz in 1596, was promoted Vice-Admiral in 1603, and in 1604 became Treasurer to the Navy. He was one of the patentees named in the patent of 1615 and in 1618 sold the office of Treasurer to concentrate on the glass trade. His first wife, who was somewhat older than himself, had died some time before 1617, for in that year he married Elizabeth Roper, a lady-in-waiting to Queen Anne, wife of James I. Elizabeth proved to be a capable businesswoman, looking after his interests whenever he had to be absent. At first sight it might seem strange that an officer in the Navy should become involved in business matters. It is recorded that even James I was moved to wonder that Robert Mansell 'should fall from water to tamper with fire'. However, I feel that there were not such sharp distinctions in those days between serving the crown, one's country, or one's own interests. The idea of naval vessels plundering foreign ships for material gain was still commonplace and the navy would have been closely involved in setting up and maintaining business interests in newly discovered parts of the world. With this in mind it is not so unlikely that Mansell's naval service had developed his business instinct and that he would avail himself of an opportunity to make a business investment with a view to financial gain.

After the granting of the patent of 1615 he apparently found difficulty in getting his partners to agree to a concerted plan of action, so he bought them all out on the promise of paying each of them an annuity of £200. At this time the two glasshouses operating under his patent were still suffering competition from wood-burning glasshouses, he had liabilities of £2800 per annum incurred by the partners of the earlier monopolies to settle earlier litigation, and in addition he had to deal with his glassmaking craftsmen while knowing nothing of the practical side of the industry himself. Starting from this unlikely beginning it is a measure of his determination and tenacity that he managed to control the glass industry in Britain for the next twenty-seven years.

With the introduction of coal firing, it became advantageous to set up the glasshouses near the sources of coal, or at sites to which coal could easily be transported. This led initially to the establishment of glasshouses in Dorset where there was shale coal, the West Midlands, in Staffordshire, Shropshire, Notts and Newcastle. Problems arose over the cost of transporting the finished product to the principal markets, and eventually production settled in places where transport of either coal to the glasshouses or the finished product to the markets was cheapest. Since transport by sea was cheapest, this effectively meant that glassmaking settled near large ports such as Bristol, London (where it had been practised since le Carré) and Newcastle. It is recorded that the cost of shipping window glass to London from Newcastle was half that of carrying it from Nottingham to London.

Mansell's method was to licence independent glassmakers to set up glasshouses to manufacture window glass or vessel glass on payment of royalties, and usually with restrictions as to where their products could be sold. Most of his licensees were the descendants of the same Norman and Lorraine glassmakers who had settled around Chiddingfold in the mid-sixteenth century. The Hennezells, the Tyzacks and Titterys had spread slowly westwards and northwards to find security of operation and supplies of fuel. Under Mansell's monopoly most of them seemed to be amenable to adopting the new method and thus they became the founders of the new trade in Stourbridge and Newcastle. Not all of them gave in so easily, and the whole period of Mansell's efforts to control the industry was punctuated by lawsuits against those who wanted freedom to continue the use of wood-fired furnaces or unrestricted opportunities to trade. Isaac Bungar was probably the most persistent of these, and he continued the fight against Mansell until his death in 1643. He lived just long enough to see Mansell's monopoly revoked by Parliament in 1642, the year in which the Civil War began.

The changing mood of the country, when the Commons became independent of the Crown, was against the idea of monopolies based on privilege and personal advantage. The Civil War finally put an end to the system of monopolies, Mansell applied unsucessfully for an extension of his patent in 1652, but continued in production at the glasshouses he had set up in London and Newcastle until his death.

We have seen how the manufacturing side of the industry

had become organised throughout the country under one hand. It consisted, though, of two distinct sections, those for window glass and for vessel glass. In due course the retailers of both these commodities also considered it advantageous to organise themselves into Guilds. Window glass manufacture went back to the earliest days of recorded glassmaking in this country, so it is not surprising that the retailers of window glass had formed themselves into the Glaziers Company in the early fourteenth century.

With the rise of Venetian glass in the sixteenth century and the growth of fine glassmaking in London, the retailers of drinking glass and mirrors also felt the need to organise themselves. They felt that in speaking with one voice they could better contest the ever-increasing taxes being levied on them and the harm which they felt travelling hawkers of glass were doing to their business and reputation. In 1635 they petitioned the King and were granted a charter for the incorporation of the Glass Sellers Company, but the Court of Aldermen of the City of London, for some reason, refused to enrol them as a Guild. It was not until after the restoration of Charles II in 1664 that they were finally enrolled. Their charter gave members of the Company exclusive rights to sell vessel glass and mirrors and the powers to prosecute the travelling hawkers. Their main complaint against these being that they sold poor quality glass and thus brought the trade into disrepute, although it is more likely that having few overheads they sold glass very much more cheaply than the Glass Sellers. The Glass Sellers Company grew steadily in influence and ultimately succeeded the monopolists in the power they exercised over the glass trade. I mention this at some length because, as we shall see, the Glass Sellers Company has an important part to play in the next stage of our story.

It finally remains to consider what sort of glassware was made during the period of Mansell's monopoly. Our attribution to Verzelini of the glasses referred to earlier depends on the fact that they are engraved with dates and names which are obviously English, and Verzelini's monopoly meant that no-one else in England should have been making glass of this type. Unfortunately, no glasses survive of the Mansell period with the same identifying decoration. In Mansell's crystal glasshouses the styles produced, and most of the workmen, were Venetian, so although complete specimens may survive, they are what would generally be termed 'façon de Venise', i.e. a style derived from Venice but adapted to the taste of Northern Europe, and made widely throughout that area. However, we know something of the types of glasses which Mansell made, because of a document he presented to the House of Lords in about 1635. This lists certain types of drinking glasses, giving the prices he charged, to show how he had kept prices down. They include:

Ordinary drinking glasses for beer	4 shillings per dozen.
Ditto for wine	2/6d. per dozen.
Cristall beer glasses–formerly bought from Venice to sell at 20/- and 24/- per dozen	Now sold for 10/- and 11/- per dozen.
Ditto wine glasses brought from Venice and sold at 18/- per dozen	Now sold at 7/- and 8/- per dozen.

The 'cristall' glasses would be those made in London in the 'façon de Venise' using soda derived from barilla which had been imported into the country since the days when John le Carré set up his first glasshouse to produce 'cristallo'. 'Ordinary glasses' were obviously of an inferior quality because of the great discrepancy in price, but they were still presumably some form of 'cristall', since he states later in the same document that he had let the rights for making 'green' glasses to a 'gentleman of known experience'. Glasses made from a potash glass similar to that produced by the Wealden glass-makers were commonly referred to as green glass.

1660-1700

During the period of the Commonwealth up to the restoration of the monarchy in 1660 the Puritan outlook of the administration was against any form of frivolity and display. Glassmaking retreated to a purely utilitarian craft and the market for the elaborate 'façon de Venise' glasses disappeared.

With the restoration of Charles II the social climate soon altered, and, encouraged by the court, style, fashion and novelty were soon evident. Following the tradition of James I and Charles I monopoly patents were still to be obtained by members of the court, and the first to obtain such a licence was the second Duke of Buckingham. The Duke appears to have acted as a middleman, putting up capital and taking his cut as a percentage of the profits. He acted in this way first in 1660 for John de la Cam, a Frenchman, for Martin Clifford and Thomas Powlden in 1661 and for Thomas Tilson in 1662. The Duke then obtained a licence to make mirror glass in 1663 and set up a glasshouse at Vauxhall which was managed by an Englishman, John Bellingham. In this way he nominally had a controlling interest in the industry, but not the complete domination achieved by Mansell. His patents expired in 1674, which date coincides with the appearance of the man who effected the third and greatest turning point in our story, George Ravenscroft. I suspect that his importance has as much to do with the changing times and the new spirit of enquiry as with any actual demand for a new material.

Along with the resurgence of style under Charles II came an awakening interest in scientific matters. The Royal Society had been founded in 1662 and its members, of many different disciplines, met to promote scientific research and enquiry. Among its members was Doctor Christopher Merrett who translated from the Italian what was probably the most important book on glassmaking *L'Arte Vitrearia*, written by Antonio Neri and published in 1612. That it had to wait fifty years for an English edition is strange, since it would surely have helped to educate English glassmakers to the trade during those years when such an objective had been so important to the English industry. Whether the publication of this book played any part or not, there seems to have been developed between 1660 and 1674 a better quality of glass which was generally described as English crystal.

There appears in a series of bills for glass supplied to the Duke of Bedford between 1650 and 1690 several types of glass which are referred to specifically by name, i.e. Venice glass, crystal, English crystal, flint, single flint and double flint. These bills cover the period during which Ravenscroft's new glass of lead was introduced. I shall have more to say about the 'flint' glasses later, but the crystal glasses are very much of the Restoration period.

Much of the glass described as Venice glass was supplied by London glass seller John Greene, who was initially in business with Michael Measey at Cary House, Strand, and later on his own at No. 10 Poultry. His invoices cover the period 1669 to 1675. Venice glasses continued to be supplied by another glass seller, Thomas Apthorpe, until 1686.

There is a further connection between John Greene, the Bedford bills and Venetian glass in a series of letters which have survived written by Greene to his glass supplier in Venice, one Alessio Morelli. In this correspondence Greene gives exact specifications for the glasses he orders, complains generally about the quality and that the goods he receives bear no relation to his orders, and on several occasions is not above giving instructions as to the method of packing his goods and the falsification of invoices with the obvious intention of

7 A late seventeenth century 'façon de Venise' wine glass. It has a funnel bowl on a hollow true baluster stem and a folded foot. This is similar to the style of glass that John Greene was buying from Alessio Morelli in the 1660's.

8 A Venetian wine glass of the late sixteenth century. It has a tall waisted bell bowl over a merese and hollow inverted baluster stem and folded foot. This has more of the character of Venice about it than does the preceding wine glass.

evading customs duty on their arrival in London. There also survive several sheets of drawings of the glasses which Greene ordered from Venice. It is noticeable that these patterns are practically all for plain glasses of generous capacity, avoiding the excesses of decoration which Venetian glass was prone to; the serpentine stems, pincered trails and elaborate moulding. These are sometimes referred to as 'Greene's glasses', not to be confused with the term 'green glass' which refers to the cheap potash glass made generally throughout England up to that period.

In a letter of 3 May 1671 Greene writes to Morelli: 'Sir, I pray you once again to take such care that I may have good, and be used very kindly in the price, else it will not be in my interest to send to Venice for neither drinking glasses nor looking glasses, for we make now very good drinking glasses in England and better looking glasses than any that comes from Venice'.

This would seem to imply that the prices Greene was paying for glass shipped from Venice were sufficiently below the prices of London-made glass that he was prepared to put up with the inconveniences of doubtful quality, breakage *en route* and the disregarding of his specifications.

The use of the word 'crystal' on the invoices undoubtedly refers to the 'façon de Venise' glasses made in London since the time of le Carré. These glasses, made by craftsmen reared in the Venetian tradition and from materials used in the Venetian product, were the domestic equivalent of the glasses which Greene and others were importing from Venice.

The description 'English Crystal' appears in the invoices for a short period between 1669 and 1672, while the term 'crystal' appears on the earliest in 1652 and continues until 1691. Since an invoice of 1674 bears the words 'Flint christalline' and 'flint' comes into common usage on the invoices from 1675 onwards, it seems as if 'flint' replaces 'English crystal'. We know that 'flint' is a term used to describe Ravenscroft's newly developed lead glass. If 'English crystal' was different from 'crystal' and bearing in mind the sequence of dates, is it possible that 'English crystal' was a transitional development which was either created by Ravenscroft in his bid for a new metal, or used by him as a stepping stone for his own researches? One of his workmen named Da Costa had apparently introduced him to the use, as his source of silica, white quartz pebbles imported from the region of the River Po in Italy. With this thought in mind let us have a closer look at what is known about Ravenscroft and his contribution to English glassmaking.

George Ravenscroft For many years it had been assumed that George Ravenscroft was born the second son of George Ravenscroft in 1618 at Sholton in the parish of Hawarden in Flintshire, dying in 1681. However, in an interesting paper presented to the Glass Circle in 1974 Rosemary Rendel suggests that he was in fact the second son of James Ravenscroft of Huntingdonshire, born in 1632, dying in 1683. This George is known to have been a merchant, to have had trading links with Venice and to have been involved in dealing in glass. He sounds a much more likely candidate to be the owner of a glasshouse at the Savoy in 1663. Nothing is known of how he got into the operative business of glassmaking, but by April 1674 he had made sufficient progress to approach the Glass Sellers Company with examples of 'a particular sort of chrystal-line Glass resembling rock crystall, not formerly exercised or used in our Kingdome'. He had also taken the precaution of applying for a patent in March 1674 before approaching the Glass Sellers. This was granted in May of that year for a period of seven years, and the Glass Sellers Company was sufficiently interested to offer him the use of a glasshouse at Henley-on-Thames. There is evidence that he experienced problems with his new metal, since there are references to crizzling and decay by Dr. Robert Plot, a Fellow of the Royal Society, who visited him at Henley, and by the Glass Sellers when they issued their Certificate of Merit in June 1676. Crizzling, which is a fine crazing and deterioration of the surface of glass, had to do with the porportions of his ingredients, and it can be assumed that it was during the resolution of these problems that he introduced lead oxide into the mixture. The use of lead in glass was known to the Venetians and since it is referred to in Neri's book – and remember that because this was only translated in 1662 it would have recently become available to English glassmakers. Very probably it was read by Ravenscroft.

By 1676 he had managed to produce a sufficiently stable metal in a manner consistent enough to encourage the Glass Sellers Company to issue a certificate of merit, which I give with the spelling modernised:

'We underwritten, do certify and attest that the defect of the flint glasses (which were formerly observed to crizzle and decay) have been redressed several months ago and the glass since made have all proved durable and lasting as any glasses whatsoever. Moreover that the usual trials wherewith the assay of glasses are made have been often reiterated on these new flint glasses with entire success and easy to be done again by anybody, which proofs the former glass would not

9 A bowl, diameter 11¾ inches, that shows signs of crizzling. This piece dates from 1675-80. The Museum of London.

undergo, besides the distinction of sound discernible by any person whatsoever. London 3 June 1676.'

This document is signed by the Clerk to the Glass Sellers Company, Samuel Moore, who had been instructed by the Company to liaise with Ravenscroft, and by Hawley Bishop. Hawley Bishop was a member of the Glass Sellers Company and had for some time before the date of the above certificate been working with Ravenscroft at Henley, so was in a position to be sure that the problem of crizzling had been cured.

The certificate enables us to draw several conclusions about Ravenscroft's progress towards his lead glass. If we can assume that he had been satisfied with his new glass to such an extent that he took out his patent and approached the Glass Sellers in 1674 it is likely that the crizzling problem occurred only after his removal to Henley. So his experiments continued while he was there. Since the Glass Sellers were interested in his progress (they undertook to sell his whole output), if the problems started at Henley they would surely have been aware of them, and it is reasonable to assume that they would be sufficiently concerned to put one of their own members (Hawley Bishop) into the glasshouse to supervise progress. Since this certificate was published several times in the London Gazette, and its general tone appears to be to reassure customers who may have had trouble with glasses they had bought, it would appear that the Glass Sellers had already been selling Ravenscroft's glass before 1676. Since the certificate says (in June 1676) that the trouble had been corrected 'several months ago' and Ravenscroft had not started in business at Henley until some time after April 1674, the problem of crizzling must have been one which made itself apparent fairly quickly in finished glasses. It is unlikely that the problem lasted more than one year. In fact, Dr. Plot, visiting Ravenscroft at Henley in April 1676, commented on the quality of the glass he was then producing.

In October and November of 1676 the London Gazette carried notices stating that Ravenscroft was permitted to mark his glassware with a seal bearing the mark of a raven's head. This must have been some form of guarantee of quality since the Glass Sellers (in an effort to restore confidence among their customers?) offered raven's head items with the offer 'no crizzling or money returned'.

In 1677 Ravenscroft agreed a price list and a further three-year contract with the Glass Sellers for the items he was supplying to them from Henley, and also by this time his Savoy glasshouse. It includes glasses for beer, claret, sacks and brandy at prices from 6d. to 1/8d.

For some reason unknown, Ravenscroft gave six months notice to terminate this contract in August 1678. Rosemary Rendel suggests that this was linked with the fact that Ravenscroft was a Catholic and the political climate at that time was unfavourable towards Catholics. His patent still had nearly three years to run, however, and although he no longer had any legal tie with the Glass Sellers, as long as he was in business making glass he would have had to deal with them. He appears to have given up work at the Savoy in 1681 or early in 1682 since in February 1682 the Glass Sellers signed a fresh agreement with Hawley Bishop for twenty-one years to continue work at the Savoy glasshouse, the property then being referred to as 'late in the occupation of George Ravenscroft Gent'n.'

That Ravenscroft was the first glassmaker to use lead in some form, although it is not mentioned specifically in either the patent or any surviving correspondence with the Glass Sellers Company, is supported by the fact that the sealed pieces which have survived are of lead glass and must have been produced between 1677 and 1679. The term which is generally used when referring to this lead glass is 'flint', qualified by 'single flint' or 'double flint'. (See the Duke of Bedford invoices and the 'Certificate of Merit' already referred to.) Houghton, in one of his *Letters for the Improvement of Commerce & Trade* in 1696 states, 'I remember the time when . . . Mr. Ravenscroft first made the flint glasses'.

I feel this use of the word flint for lead glass deserves some explanation. In an effort to improve the quality of the crystal glassware made in London from the mid-sixteenth century onwards, various methods and materials had been used to improve the quality of the product. From le Carré onwards the

10 An English glass decanter jug from the seventeenth century. Fitzwilliam Museum, Cambridge.

soda derived from Spanish barilla had been imported into London. Various forms and sources of silica had been tried. One of these was calcined flint; that is, it was first burned in a furnace and crushed to a white powder. This had produced some improvement, and according to Dr. Plot this is the material which Ravenscroft was using before he was introduced to the white Italian quartz by Da Costa. There is little doubt that the public was aware of and accustomed to good quality glassware based on flint, and that the term flint would be associated with a high standard. Merrett, on p.261 of *The Art of Glass* (a translation of Neri), 'Flints indeed have all the properties, and when calcined, powdered and ferced (sieved) into a most impalpable powder, make incomparable pure and white crystal metal.' The addition of lead to the glass was initially a commercial secret, so the product containing it could easily be represented as being a better type of flint glass. We see from the Duke of Bedford invoices that 'flint glass' was being supplied from March 1676 onwards, when invoices refer to 'new flint wine glasses'. The term also seems to have been adopted by the glasshouses. From this time on, glasshouses are defined as being 'flint glasshouses' making vessel glass for domestic use, or 'bottle glasshouses'.

The term flint glass survived right to the end of the nineteenth century when firms such as Sowerbys in Gateshead, mass-producing pressed glass, still used the word to denote any of their products in clear glass as opposed to coloured glass, although by this time there was no lead in the glass at all.

The terms 'single' and 'double' flint were used to denote glasses of differing weight. In fact before these terms became popular, glasses were described as being thin or thick. This, I think, gives us the clue to their true meaning. Since glass was commonly sold by weight, a hangover from the days when window glass was the principal product of the glass industry, the thickness of the glass determined the price. Among the Woburn Abbey invoices there are many recording both single flint glasses and double flint glasses, the prices for the latter being exactly twice the prices for the former.

All the evidence so far discovered points, I think, to the conclusion that lead was first introduced into glassmaking in this country to act as a stabilising agent and to solve the problems of crizzling in glass. It is not clear how much lead Ravenscroft introduced initially, but over the years following his discovery the lead content increased until as much as 37% by volume was being used.

The great benefit of the use of lead was to produce a glass of greater transparency, whiter colour and with greater refractive properties than the Venetian 'cristallo' which rendered it highly suitable for articles of cut glass. It was also a softer material, which was to make it attractive to the glass decorators, particularly the great Dutch engravers of the mid-eighteenth century. For the first time glass of considerable thickness could be made which retained the transparency of the very thinly blown Venetian 'cristallo'. This new material was prized as much abroad as at home, and considerable quantities were exported to Europe and later to North America. In view of its popularity and its rapid adoption among the glasshouses of the British Isles it surprises me that it was not equally rapidly taken up in Europe. There are one or two references to attempts to produce the English crystal in Europe. In Spain as early as 1720 and in Germany a little later, but they were apparently unsuccessful, and it is not until 1784 that there is a reliable record of lead crystal being produced in France. I think this is probably tied in with the fact that Continental glasshouses stuck to their wood-fired furnaces for so long after coal was generally used in this country.

Ravenscroft imported Italian glassmakers to run his glasshouses and the earliest lead glass shows strong evidence of this Venetian influence. Surviving articles in glass dating to about 1685 have blown quatrefoil knops, pincered wings, applied trailing and other features typical of Venice. But this new glass of lead had noticeably different handling qualities from the light Venetian soda glass, and did not really lend itself to the elaborate decorative techniques of that tradition. By 1690 lead glass was being widely used in Britain and the rapid increase in production began which was to bring the use of glass table ware to an ever-increasing market. This increase must have demanded a corresponding increase in the number of glassmakers, and more and more English men undoubtedly entered the trade. Thus the transfer of the glass industry from foreign craftsmen, who guarded their secrets jealously, through the English monopolists and the Glass Sellers Company was finally completed when the craftsmen themselves were predominantly English. The combination of these three factors, a new metal, a new breed of glassmakers and a wider public, all tended to turn fashion away from the effusiveness of Venice and to create a truly English style which was to make English glass the most important in the world for the next hundred years. The next chapters deal with the development of this style.

Chapter 2
Styles of eighteenth century drinking glasses

As far as the collector of English glass is concerned, the narrative so far can only be of academic interest. So little glass made prior to 1690 survives today that there is hardly sufficient to form a worthwhile collection, and prices of early pieces are beyond the means of almost all private collectors. Before the advent of Ravenscroft, good quality glassware was made in a very few glasshouses for a wealthy but limited clientele. From 1690 onwards the quantity that has survived is relatively plentiful and varied, two essentials to any form of collecting. This, then, is the period which is of most interest to collectors, and it is fortunate that the progression of styles throughout the eighteenth century was both orderly and well documented. Briefly, the knopping of the baluster stemmed glasses of the early eighteenth century gave way to the plain stems of the middle of the century. These were followed by the air and opaque twist stemmed glasses of the third quarter of the

11, 12 Thomas Pelham-Holles, 1st Duke of Newcastle, with his nephew Henry Clinton, Earl of Lincoln and later the 2nd Duke of Newcastle. The glasses are drawn trumpet bowls on baluster stems (see enlargement). The painting is by Godfrey Kneller, *c.* 1721, and was painted for the Kit Kat Club. National Portrait Gallery, London.

century, which in turn were succeeded by the facet stems of the late eighteenth century. Before considering these styles in detail it would be appropriate, I think, to explain a number of the terms used in describing old glass which will occur in the ensuing chapters and some of the hallmarks of old glass which will help to identify it.

Explanation of terms

One of the most difficult things for the novice in old glassware to do is to describe satisfactorily the style, shape and character of a piece of glass to anyone else. This generally seems to be accomplished with much hand waving and vague references to the owner's ancestors. There are, however, a number of descriptive terms and expressions which are generally used between knowledgeable people.

13 A goblet *c.* 1690-1700, 12 inches in height. British Museum, London.

Until the last few years of the eighteenth century, drinking glasses were composed of three elements: the bowl, the stem and the foot. Each of these elements could be in a variety of shapes, each of which has its own name. The two diagrams show all the important shapes of bowls. Knops are shaped sections decorating the stem, and where they are sufficiently well defined they may be referred to by name. The later glasses generally have knops which are nothing more than swellings in the stem, so they may be referred to as base, shoulder or centre knops. Air twist and opaque glasses are known with up to five knops, and the more knops there are, the rarer is the glass. Where there are one or two knops these are usually in the middle of the stem or at the top, i.e. centre or shoulder knops. Glasses with base knops only are uncommon. Another line drawing on page 47 shows all the major knop shapes.

Although I have said that glasses have three elements, most drinking glasses are described as being two- or three-piece glasses. A two-piece glass is one in which the bowl and stem are made from one piece or 'gather' (see below) of glass, with the foot made separately. A three-piece glass is made from three separate pieces of glass. As a general rule all glasses with drawn trumpet or bell bowls on plain or air twist stems are two-piece glasses, while glasses with any other bowl shape, and all opaque twist glasses are three-piece glasses. Three-piece air and opaque twist glasses can usually be detected because the pattern ends abruptly where the stem meets the bowl. Three-piece plain stem glasses can usually be detected by holding the glass at an angle to the light and by looking up the stem towards the bowl a slight change in the reflection of the light across the joint may be seen.

32

14 A wine glass *c.* 1730. It is 7 inches in height and has a moulded trumpet bowl on a domed and folded foot. Pilkington Glass Museum, St Helens.

15 The typical *Y* mark left by the 'gadget' which was used as an alternative to the pontil iron during the nineteenth century.

Heavy baluster, light baluster and Newcastle baluster stems are often made in several sections, according to how many knops there are. Such glasses may be four, five or even six-piece glasses.

The 'gather' is the amount of glass taken from the glass pot, and from which the vessel is to be made. The glass is commonly referred to as 'metal'. This has always been the trade term for it and probably takes its origin from the similarity of molten glass in the glass pot to any molten metal in its crucible.

The foot

The foot is generally the most informative part of the glass when age and authenticity are in question. It is my belief that whenever a glassmaker has copied an earlier style, no matter how accurate the bowl and stem may be, the foot is always made in a manner appropriate to the period in which he is working. Briefly, the feet of glasses made in the first half of the eighteenth century have fairly highly conical feet, well defined pontil marks and the majority have folded rims. Later in the century the feet tended to be thicker, flatter and folded rims virtually disappear. By 1800 more and more feet have ground pontil marks. The feet of these eighteenth century glasses usually show distinct circumferential flow lines and have a very slight irregular under surface. By the mid-nineteenth century the feet are once again fairly thin, have a very smooth under surface and many good quality glasses are star cut underneath. The pontil is almost invariably ground out. By the late nineteenth century and into the twentieth century the pontil mark disappears entirely, the under surface is very smooth and free from flow lines. Frequently there is a shaped profile so that the edge of the foot is not in contact with whatever surface the glass stands on.

During the early years of the nineteenth century many small wine glasses, up to about 4 inches in height, were made with folded feet. It is commonly thought that any glass with a folded foot must be eighteenth century, but this is not so. The style of the glass must be taken into account when assessing age.

There is one other characteristic mark to be found on the underside of the feet of glasses. This is a capital *T* or *Y* mark impressed into a flat foot with no sign of a pontil mark. This was caused by a springloaded instrument, called a 'gadget', that succeeded the pontil iron as a means of holding the glass while it was finished off. It was much easier to use, since the glass was not firmly fixed to it as it was to the pontil iron. Occasionally one may see two parallel lines on the upper surface of the foot, either side of the stem, where the arms of the gadget pressed into the still soft glass.

The folded foot was inherited from Venetian glassmaking. The fine 'cristallo' of the Venetians was generally very thinly blown, and as the foot was also blown, extra strength was required at its edge to prevent it being damaged. This was achieved by turning the rim to produce what was, in effect, a hem. English glassmakers continued this practice for a long time until the thicker foot became popular, when the extra strength that was inherent in this type of foot obviated the need for a folded edge. The wisdom of all this is apparent if you stand several eighteenth century glasses side by side. When touching each other it will be seen that the edges of the feet come into contact first, the bowls not touching at all. Now try the same thing with modern glasses. This time the sides of the bowls will touch first. Although this fact gives modern glasses that difference of balance which is one of the main contrasts between the twentieth and eighteenth centuries, to have bowls in contact is more practical since these glasses are less likely to get damaged. The edges of the feet of antique glasses coming into contact with each other must have been the major cause of damage to them.

The pontil mark

This, I find, is another very common factor in the mis-dating of drinking glasses. The pontil mark, a circular rough mark in the centre of the underside of the foot, is only a sign of the method by which the glass was made. If a glass is made in that fashion today, and most handmade glasses are, then it will have a pontil mark. It is the practice nowadays to remove it by grinding and polishing, but that does not alter the principle. Since practically all glass in the eighteenth century was finished on a pontil iron I expect such glass to show signs of this. Therefore eighteenth century glass should show evidence of the use of a pontil iron, but signs of the use of a pontil iron does not of itself guarantee that a glass is antique.

The ground pontil became necessary as the eighteenth century gave way to the nineteenth, and the feet of glasses were made progressively flatter. Unground, the mark could protrude and prevent the glass sitting properly on a flat surface. In glasses of high quality it would also be normal to give a glass that extra finish by polishing out the pontil mark. The earliest evidence I have come across of this practice dates from about 1760.

16 A toasting glass c. 1760. It consists of a drawn trumpet bowl on a tall slender plain stem and a plain foot.

The bowl

Most modern glasses are blown into moulds, even those made by hand on a blowing iron. This produces the desired shape consistently without the need for hand finishing. The interior of the mould will have an almost mirror finish so that the finished product will have a similar surface. Antique glasses which were free blown and then shaped by hand exhibit several characteristics which are different from modern ones. Since the glass did not take its smoothness from a mould there are usually striations and flow lines visible in the glass. These are usually more or less at right angles to the vertical axis. When the bubble forming the bowl was cut from the blowing iron with a pair of shears it nearly always left a mark which can be detected by either a slight step in the rim or a slight thickening of the edge at the point of separation. However slight these may be they can usually be detected by turning the glass around against the light. The other sign of a handmade glass is the presence of marks in the bowl which are generally parallel to the vertical axis and were caused by the tool with which the glassmaker produced the finished shape of the bowl. Again, these can generally only be seen by looking through the glass from the inside of the bowl, whilst turning it against the light. These marks tend to be more noticeable in thinly blown

17 Three plain stem wine glasses all with folded feet c. 1750. (Left) An engraved ogee bowl. (Centre) A drawn trumpet bowl with a plain air stem containing an air tear. (Right) A bell bowl.

glasses of the first half of the eighteenth century and are less often seen as the century progresses.

Some glasses with elaborately moulded patterns on the bowl have poor definition at either the rim or the base. This is because as the glass is inflated into the mould the temperature drops and the glass becomes less plastic. Since the rate of expansion was limited by the power of human lungs, the glass blower would not always have enough strength to produce a clear impression over the whole surface of the mould. The first part to come into contact with the pattern while it is still hot picks up a good impression; the last part making contact may be indistinct. It depends so much on the skill of the blower.

Colour and impurities

Another topic we need to examine, and one which is open to much discussion and different interpretations amongst collectors, is the relevance and importance of colour in old glass.

Although Ravenscroft's glass was noted by Dr. Plot as being 'hard, durable and whiter than any from Venice' it would not compare in clarity with modern crystal glass. The state of chemical knowledge in the late seventeenth and early eighteenth centuries was such that the impurities in silica which produce the tints could not be properly controlled or accurately removed. I am sure that every glassmaker's ambition was to produce a glass which was white and clear and every so often a batch would be melted that produced such a glass. In the great majority of cases, however, a wide variety of black, green, yellow and blue tints occurs in old glassware. The tint in

18 *Above:* Three dram glasses. (Left) An ovoid bowl on a plain stem and oversewn foot, *c*. 1750. (Centre) An engraved round bowl on a plain stem and foot, *c*. 1750. (Right) A ribbed ovoid bowl and stem on a plain foot, *c*. 1770.

Opposite: **Bowl shapes of drinking glasses** (Part one).
1, 2 The narrowest and widest variations of round funnel bowls.
3 The round funnel bowl of an ale glass.
4 The round funnel bowl of a Continental glass. Its sides are more parallel than 3 and has a fuller base.
5, 6 The narrowest and widest variations in wine glasses of ogee bowls.
7 Ogee bowl of an ale glass.
8 A double ogee or pan-type bowl.
9 A double ogee or saucer-topped bowl.
10 A double ogee or cup-topped bowl. This occurs rarely on baluster stem glasses.
11 A shallow-lipped double ogee bowl. This is most commonly found on sweetmeat glasses.

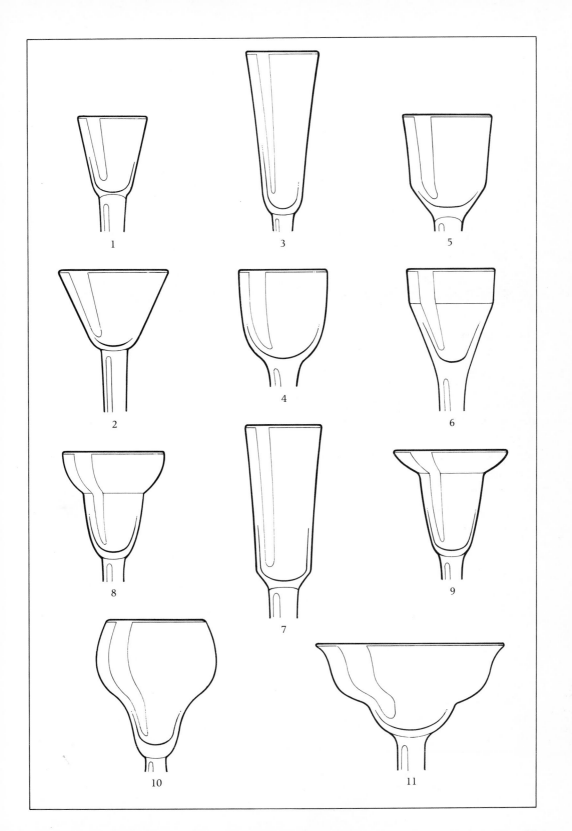

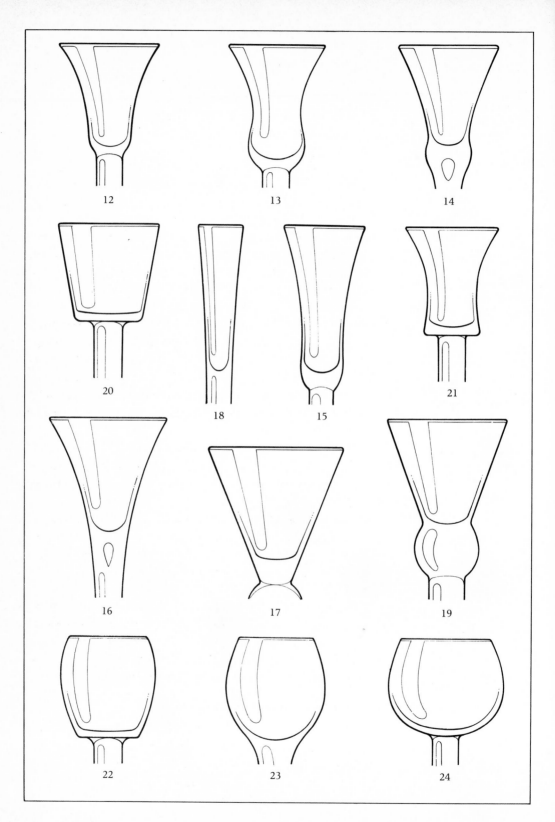

Opposite: **Bowl shapes of drinking glasses** (Part two).

12 A bell bowl.
13 A waisted bell bowl.
14 An intermediate form of bell bowl midway between the drawn trumpet bowl and the true bell bowl. It is solid at its base and usually has an air tear.
15 A bell bowl of an ale glass.
16 One of the most common forms of drawn trumpet bowl.
17 A straight-sided funnel bowl.
18 A narrow drawn trumpet bowl. This rare shape usually occurs on ratafia glasses.
19 A thistle bowl, usually solid at the base.
20 A bucket bowl.
21 A waisted bucket bowl.
22 A barrel bowl. This is most commonly found in the nineteenth century.
23 An ovoid bowl.
24 A cup bowl, most often found on mead glasses.

any particular glass, viewed in isolation, is not always easy to see, but if several are stood side by side the differences are much more apparent.

Some people consider that green or yellow tints are an indication that a glass is made of soda glass rather than lead glass. While soda glasses are frequently of these colours, it is not necessarily true. I have seen English soda glasses of as clear a colour as any lead glass, and lead glass of a distinct green hue. While these undesirable colours could be corrected with the use of neutralising agents (manganese was the commonest of these), the problem was minimised by using sand of the highest known purity. Kings Lynn in Norfolk was one of the best sources, and sand from this region was shipped to most glassmaking areas. Many collectors consider a black or blue tint in antique glass to be desirable, and quite a lot of early baluster stem glasses are of a dark metal. All of this means that the newcomer to glass collecting faces a problem when attempting to tell lead glass from soda glass. The surest way is to apply ultra-violet light to the glass, when soda glass will give off a strong yellowish green reflection, while lead glass shines with a purple light. Until recently ultra-violet lights were bulky and expensive, but there are now several lightweight battery powered lamps on the market so that such a test may be conveniently be carried out anywhere.

By the latter part of the eighteenth century technical and chemical improvements ensured that the metal used was of a high quality and glass from that time onwards became consistently whiter and clearer.

In many glasses of the eighteenth century one can see small lumps of foreign matter which are usually referred to as seeds. These are either pieces of undissolved raw materials or impurities from the furnace finding their way into the glass pot.

In assessing the genuineness of early glass, any or all of these faults or signs may be present. The presence or absence of any one is not sufficient to prove the glass genuine or otherwise, but an examination taking account of all the factors I have mentioned is essential to arrive at a correct appraisal.

Proportion, weight and sound

Proportion and balance are other factors to be considered in assessing old glass, but this is difficult to explain. I am sure it is a skill acquired by looking at many glasses over a long period. I will have more to say about this when discussing fakes and reproductions. I occasionally see a glass which I know instinctively is not true to its apparent period, but am not able to say why without detailed examination. Another dilemma facing the newcomer to glass collecting is how to tell lead glass from soda glass. In the previous section I discussed how to do this by using ultra-violet light, but as an alternative one can resort to more elementary tests. Given two glasses of about the same size, the lead glass example will generally be noticeably heavier than its soda glass counterpart. With some experience one develops an idea of what the weight of a glass will be on picking it up. Soda glass invariably feels lighter than one expects. It is for this reason that the novice should handle as many pieces of glassware as possible, since it is by this means that one comes to judge weight, texture and balance; all factors that enable a correct assessment to be made of antique glassware.

As I have already mentioned, soda glass is often of a noticeable yellowish green tint, but this should never be taken as proof one way or the other on its own. The other factor one may wish to distinguish lead from soda is that of the ring or sound of a glass. Lead glass vessels usually give off a clear ringing sound when lightly struck. This sound depends very much on the size and thickness of the glass, but with large, thinly blown items the sound can be like that of a bell, continuing for a minute or more. Soda glass, on the other hand, produces either a dull thud or a sharp sound which dies away almost instantly when struck in the same way. This, like the other points mentioned, is not infallible since a short, thick lead glass is inflexible and will not produce the characteristic ring. It is rather a combination of all these points which will enable one to differentiate lead from soda; weight, colour, sound. One final comment; be circumspect when striking glass which is not yet yours, it is quite fragile.

Returning to our examination of eighteenth century styles in glass we begin with the period of plain baluster stemmed glasses.

Baluster stems

The expression 'baluster stem' applies to a wide variety of drinking glasses which have in common the fact that the stems are composed of one or more shaped sections which are commonly called knops. These knops are identified by different names, some of which specifically include the word baluster. Thus the word baluster is both a generic noun to cover all glasses with these knop formations and a specific word when applied to knops termed 'true' or 'inverted'

19 Three fragments of late
sixteenth or early
seventeenth century
drinking glasses. (Left) The
foot and knopped stem of a
wine glass. (Centre) The foot
rim and high kick-in base of
a tall beaker which probably
had tapering straight sides.
This style was also made in
Germany, and some
reconstructions were
produced in the 1920's by
Powell's Whitefriars
Glassworks from fragments
found in Surrey. (Right) A
wine glass base with a flat
knop. This illustration and
20 overleaf demonstrate the
varying shades of the coarse,
common glassware known as
'green' glass. Ashmolean
Museum, Oxford.

20 *Above:* Three fragments of late sixteenth or early seventeenth century glass. (Left) A wrythen bottle. (Centre) The neck of a larger wrythen bottle. (Right) The base and part of the body of a barrel-shaped beaker. Ashmolean Museum, Oxford.

21 *Opposite:* A small cream jug in amethyst glass with an applied handle. This is probably from Bristol, *c.* 1790. L. M. Bickerton Esq., Worthing.

balusters, the word baluster being an architectural term for the vertical section of a balustrade, which has a gradually changing section leading to a swelling at either the top or the base.

This group of glasses merits consideration in some detail, since they endured for about fifty years, changing their character considerably over this period. For the sake of simplicity most authorities group these as heavy baluster, light baluster and balustroid, but not everyone groups the same glasses under the same heading. Thus, what is heavy baluster in one book is light baluster in another, while different writers illustrate similar glasses under the titles light baluster and balustroid.

My own experience indicates that there is considerable overlapping of the styles and many transitional glasses which fit precisely into none of the accepted categories.

The baluster stems generally are the last demonstration of the Venetian tradition in English glassmaking. Although the glasses we are talking about–those from 1690 onwards–are very different in character from their Venetian forebears, the more or less elaborate stem formulations derive directly from that Venetian tradition. The decorative aspect of the glass is created in the making rather than in any subsequent operation. The knops of the stems take their inspiration from the elaborate blown and moulded knopped stems of Venetian glasses. Initially, however, they had a much more puritanical aspect. The earliest of the truly English baluster stems were the inverted baluster. In these we find round funnel or funnel bowls set on heavy, squat inverted baluster stems. These glasses have a proportion that marks them out from similar glasses of only ten or fifteen years later. Most of these can truly be termed 'double flint'. Some of the 'single' flint examples show even more sympathy with the Venetian style. These latter have wide, thinly blown round funnel bowls and folded feet, which have the narrowest of turning at the edge, a feature seen in most Venetian made glasses. Although the physical size and weight of these glasses can vary considerably, from 12 inches to 13 inches tall and 10 lbs. or so in weight to 5 inches and 4 to 5 ozs. or so in weight, there is a character which runs through the whole group, putting them all firmly in the category called 'heavy baluster'.

Glasses in the heavy baluster style continued in production until about 1725, and during that period a number of different knop shapes made their appearance. Most of them are self-descriptive: thus we get acorn knops, egg knops, mushroom knops and so on. Generally the stems of the heavy baluster

group consist of one knop only, with the knop forming the major part of the stem. Where there is more than one knop it is usually no more than a plain round knop at the base of the stem. The majority of glasses of this period have bowls which are solid at the base, while most feet are of the folded conical variety. Domed feet and plain feet are in the minority.

The heavy proportions of these glasses gave way to another group of baluster stemmed glasses which date generally from about 1720 to 1735. These are generally called light baluster, and again this is not so much a comment on their weight as their general proportions and character. From about 1720 drinking glasses tended to become more slender relative to their height. Where before the knop took up practically all the stem when there was only one knop involved, it now took up only part of the stem and parallel plain sections make up the rest. More importantly, stems now appear which consist of more than one knop, usually one of the types mentioned above in conjunction with an inverted or true baluster section. A popular one was the annulated knop, which consists of a series of layers

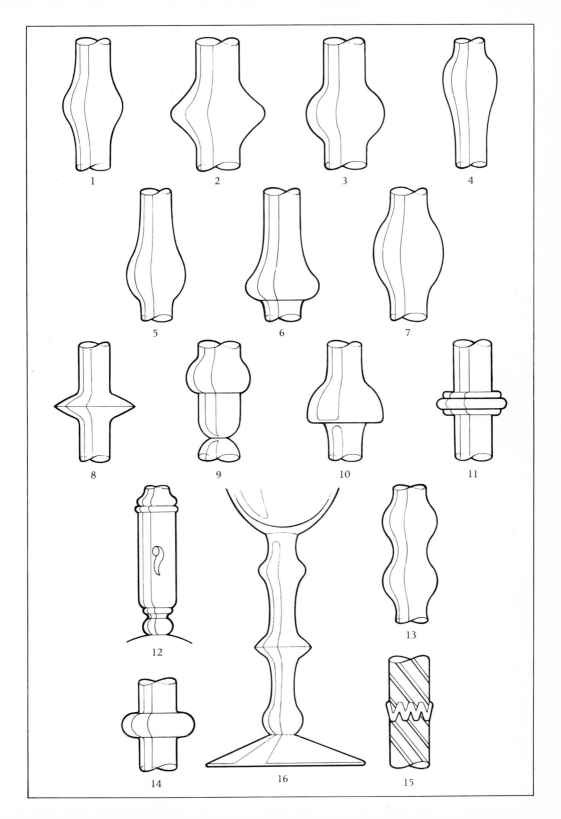

diminishing in size above and below the central one. This type, although rare in heavy baluster glasses, had as many as seven layers, but on light baluster stems it was almost always limited to three rings. While the bell bowl was occasionally met with on heavy baluster glasses, it became one of the most popular types on light balusters. The curved and flared sides of this type of bowl always seem to me to add to the lightness of the style.

These were not quite the last glasses to depend on the well defined knop formation for their decoration; that was reserved for the Newcastle light balusters which will be discussed later. For general use the light balusters gave way to the balustroid group of glasses. The name derives from the fact that although they incorporate knops in the stems the knops themselves are debased in style and usually appear as interruptions in a plain stem rather than the most important part of the stem.

Balustroids fall into three sub-divisions, and cover the period from about 1730 to 1750. The first of these is a group of glasses which still have fairly elaborately shaped stems, generally incorporating an angular knop, an inverted baluster and a base knop. However, they differ markedly from the light baluster in that the stems are usually almost hollow since they contain large and elongated air tears, the general outline is not so well defined, they lack the elegance of the true light baluster

24 *Left:* An ale glass, *c.* 1710. It consists of a tall bowl on a collar above a small spherical knop, true baluster stem and folded conical foot.

25 *Centre:* A light baluster wine glass, *c.* 1720. A bell bowl on a double drop knop stem and a folded foot.

26 *Above:* A light baluster wine glass, *c.* 1725. A bell bowl, the stem having a dumb-bell knop between two ball drop knops. There is a folded foot.

27 *Above:* A wine glass, *c.* 1740. A drawn trumpet bowl with a plain stem section over a rudimentary ball knop and a large ball knop containing air beads. There is a domed plain foot.

28 *Centre:* A light baluster wine glass, *c.* 1730. The bell bowl surmounts a collar and a true baluster stem and a base knop. There is a domed and folded foot.

29 *Right:* A sweetmeat glass, *c.* 1730. The folded rim of the double ogee bowl is decorated with loops which end in prunts. The baluster stem has an annulated knop over a plain section and a base knop. There is a domed and folded foot.

and, most noticeable, they are generally not so well made. This last characteristic is even more true of the next sub-division in the group. The glass is usually of a distinct yellow or greenish tint. It has noticeable striations or flow lines in the metal, and often contains small lumps of impurities or raw material which has not properly melted. It was as if these glasses originated in glasshouses where the operatives were not experienced, or they were quickly made for a cheap market. I am sure they all date from a relatively short period, but too many have survived for us to believe that they all came from one source. They are basically plain stemmed glasses which have one, two or three very simple or rudimentary round knops. The plain sections are often irregular and tapering. It is in this group, however, that the ogee bowl makes its appearance in any quantity. This is a straight-sided bowl with a sharp incurve at the base.

It is debatable whether the third division of this group should be related to the balustroids or the plain stems. Basically they are glasses which have similarly knopped stems to the group above, but they differ in two respects. The knops are more usually angular knops rather than round ones and the glasses are very much better made and of a better colour. This last aspect has a much closer affinity with the truly plain stem glasses which followed them. In any case this was, for all

49

practical purposes the last expression of knopped stem glasses as a general manufacture.

I mentioned earlier that there seem to be some transitional types, and the most noticeable of these are glasses that occasionally turn up which display the most obvious characteristics of both light baluster and balustroid glasses. They have well-defined knops, solid stems and good metal, but their general weight, balance and style seems to tie them in with the balustroid group. Whether they represent a step forward or the last expression of a passing style is hard to say.

Although glassmaking had firmly established itself in several provincial centres by the early eighteenth century, London was still the centre of influence and the source of taste and style. Given the conservatism of the provinces and the slowness of communication, the overlap of changing styles is understandable. What London did today would take several years before being generally adopted throughout the country. One startling exception to this, however, was a group of glasses I have already referred to in passing, the Newcastle light balusters.

By 1740 glasses with knopped stems had all but gone out of fashion, but about this time a new style of glass appeared in

30 *Above:* Three balustroid wine glasses, all with folded feet, *c.* 1740. (Left) A round funnel bowl, a stem with shoulder and centre knops. (Centre) A bell bowl, a stem with a plain section over an inverted baluster. (Right) A bell bowl with two knops.

31 *Opposite above:* A wine glass, *c.* 1740. A bell bowl surmounting an angular knop over a rudimentary inverted baluster stem.

32 *Opposite below:* Three Newcastle baluster wine glasses, all with plain feet, *c.* 1750. (Left) A round funnel bowl. Its stem has a ball knop over an inverted baluster. (Centre) A bell bowl engraved with a foliate border. The stem has four knops. (Right) A drawn trumpet bowl on a plain section over an inverted baluster stem with air beads.

which elaborately knopped stems were the most important feature. These are commonly associated with Newcastle-on-Tyne, although I can find no positive evidence for this association. In fact, books published early in this century make no connection between these glasses and Newcastle. W. A. Thorpe in his *History of English and Irish Glass* published in 1929, appears to be the first author to make the attribution, but he gives no firm evidence to support the idea. Other authors subsequently made the same connection, but again I can find no firm evidence to support the idea. There are, however, certain inferences that may be drawn as to their origin, but let us first consider what makes these glasses so distinctive. (See illustrations **32-35**.)

Whereas the average height of light baluster glasses is $6\frac{1}{2}$ inches to $6\frac{3}{4}$ inches, the 'Newcastle' type averages $7\frac{1}{2}$ inches. While the light balusters have all the standard bowl types, the Newcastle glasses have predominantly wide round funnel bowls, the remainder being mostly trumpet bowls. The metal is of a uniform whiteness and of high quality, but it is the stems which are most distinctive. They are tall and slender incorporating as many as five different knops. Air beads in the knops are a frequent feature. The quality and style are

consistent throughout the whole group. So why should they be attributed to Newcastle?

As we have shown, Newcastle was one of the important glassmaking centres of the country. It undoubtedly made all the other styles of glass as they became popular throughout the eighteenth century and there is generally nothing to distinguish the Newcastle product from that made anywhere else. The two important factors about the glasses under discussion are their uniform quality and the fact that they date from a period when baluster stems had generally gone out of fashion. By 1740 the knops of baluster stems had generally declined to become vague swellings in otherwise plain stems, but the Newcastle glasses were just making their appearance and were to continue for another twenty-five years. This suggests to me glasses made in a provincial centre rather than London, and made for a particular reason or market. It is an interesting fact that most of these glasses are engraved, and there is little doubt that most of the engraving was carried out in Holland. Inscriptions are usually in Dutch and a number of signed pieces have survived, the signatures being of well-known Dutch engravers. On closer examination it will be discovered that although these glasses are undoubtedly English, using well-

33 *Left:* A Newcastle light baluster wine glass, *c.* 1750. The round funnel bowl is engraved with Baroque foliage. The unusual composite stem has a knopped air twist section over an inverted baluster stem containing air beads. There is a small base knop and a plain foot.

34 *Above:* A Newcastle glass goblet, wheel-engraved in Holland. The inscription wishes happiness to the newly married Christina and Ysbrant Cardinaal, 18 April 1741. Pilkington Glass Museum, St Helens.

known English shapes, the overall effect is more closely allied to the Nuremberg goblets (in silver and glass) made in Germany in the fifteenth to seventeenth centuries, and 'façon de Venise' goblets made in the Netherlands during the seventeenth century. That there was a well-established trade between Newcastle and Holland in the eighteenth century is on record.

We can now build up a picture of a product being deliberately developed to satisfy a specific demand from an overseas market. All these factors would certainly tend to make Newcastle a very likely source of these glasses. One final point: there are several glasses of this group enamelled in colours by the Beilby family, who were working in Newcastle in the 1760's and 1770's. It is surely most likely that they used locally made glass.

Plain stems

Much significance has been placed by other writers on the effect of the Excise Duty imposed on glassmaking by an Act of 1745. This was introduced to raise revenue to pay for the wars being waged in Europe by George II. It consisted of a sum of 9/4d (47p) on each hundredweight of metal for making crown plate and flint glass, i.e. window glass and vessel glass, while bottle glass attracted a duty of 2/4d (12p) per hundredweight. The tax was thus levied on the metal coming from the glass pot, not the finished article, so that the specific gravity of the metal became an important consideration.

Specific gravity affects volume in relation to weight, the higher the specific gravity the lower the volume. Since lead has a high specific gravity it follows that the more lead there was in glass the smaller the volume per pound weight. As the tax was levied on weight, the glassmakers could mitigate slightly its effect by decreasing the lead content, thereby increasing the volume. This would give them more material per pound weight to turn into finished vessels. However, I do not think that this had quite so much effect on design as has been represented. The tendency towards smaller, lighter and less elaborate glasses was already well advanced before the duty was introduced. Fashion is a pendulum which swings between extremes of elaboration and plainness. It affects most things, particularly those for domestic use, and glassware was only following the trend that can be seen, for example, in furniture and silver of the same period. The excise may well have accelerated that trend, but was not, by itself, entirely responsible for it.

A type of glass occasionally turns up which has a hollow

35 A Newcastle wine glass, wheel-engraved in Holland. It bears the arms of William IV of Orange, who married Anne, daughter of George II, in 1734.

53

stem, virtually a tube between bowl and foot. These are sometimes claimed to be glasses specifically designed to defeat the excise by reducing weight to a minimum. If this was the case they should be much more common than they are in relation to other glasses of the period which have survived. In any case the practice of incorporating air into the stems of glasses had been used since the days of the heavy balusters. When a distinctive feature such as these tubular stems occurs on glasses only occasionally I am more inclined to think that it is the product of one particular glasshouse rather than something which was in widespread use by the glass trade.

By the middle of the eighteenth century plain stemmed glasses had become the most commonly produced, and the classic patterns of the period are the drawn trumpet bowl on a plain stem containing an air tear, and the bell bowl on plain stem which often contains an air tear where the bowl joins the stem. The former are widely known as 'tear glasses' although, as I have said, the idea of using air as a decorative feature in glass was by no means confined to this particular style.

By this time the capacity of stemmed drinking glasses averaged between 2 and 3 fluid ounces, and many people, on first becoming interested in eighteenth-century glass, comment on this, assuming that the contents would be much stronger than the equivalent beverages today, and that their owners therefore drank less. This is not so. Most of the glasses we collect today were made as wine glasses, and the alcoholic strength of wine was the same then as now, since it is achieved naturally. Size was dictated rather by what was considered socially correct than by the strength of the drink to be consumed. After all, it is not the amount which a glass holds which makes one drunk, but rather the number of times it is filled up. Our attitude to these small capacity glasses is influenced, I am sure, by the glasses we accept as normal today. In mid-Victorian times, by contrast, large wine glasses were made which would be considered gross today. Having said this, one does occasionally come across very large glasses all through the eighteenth century but they do not appear to have been in general use.

Silesian stems

Before we go on to examine the styles of the second half of the eighteenth century there is one group of glasses that we have not yet considered. They have tapering moulded stems and take their name from Silesia, an important glassmaking region of Germany which became Czechoslovakia after the First

36 *Opposite above left:* A wine glass, c. 1720. It comprises a round funnel bowl on a ball knop over a hollow six-sided Silesian stem and a plain foot.

37 *Opposite above centre:* A Silesian-stem wine glass. This is an example of the continental origin from which the preceding illustration derives; compare the relative proportions of the stem to the bowl.

38 *Opposite above right:* A wine glass, c. 1725. The bell bowl is on a six-sided Silesian stem and folded foot.

39 *Opposite below left:* A sweetmeat glass, c. 1740. The ribbed pan-topped bowl is on an eight-sided Silesian stem and a domed and ribbed foot.

40 *Opposite below right:* A candlestick, c. 1720. The semi-solid Silesian stem has eight sides; there are large studs on the shoulder above it, and below this are knops containing rows of tears. There are larger studs on the domed foot. Pilkington Museum of Glass, St Helens.

World War. They don't fit into the natural progression of English styles but were introduced as a compliment, to mark the accession of George I who came from Germany. They derive from a style which was common in Germany but the English glassmakers soon managed to endow it with a native character that immediately distinguishes it from its Continental original. The earliest ones had four-sided square stems and a very small number have survived which bear, in embossed letters round the shoulder the words 'God Save the King' or 'God Bless the King' and sometimes a crown as well. These commemorate the accession of George I and must therefore date from about 1714. Soon afterwards the English glassmakers modified these stems to six and eight sides. They fall into two groups. One consists of glasses of very light weight, usually having a funnel bowl on a six-sided stem, and not particularly well made. The other group is generally of very high quality, heavy, and of good colour, with several bowl shapes on both six- and eight-sided stems. They often have diamonds or stars clearly moulded at the top of each corner of the stem.

The main distinction between the English and Continental versions is that the latter are of soda metal and the bowls usually dominate the stems, which are rarely well-defined. The English glasses, even the lightweight ones, are lead glass, the

41 Three air twist glasses, all c. 1760. (Left) A drawn trumpet bowl on a multi-ply spiral air twist stem on a folded foot. (Centre) A bell bowl on a mixed-twist air stem with central air gauze surrounded by a two-strand opaque-twist spiral. There is a plain foot. (Right) A round funnel bowl on an air twist stem with shoulder and centre knops. There is a plain foot.

42 *Below:* A wine glass, *c.* 1760. The bell bowl is on an air twist stem with an applied vermicular collar. There is a plain foot. Notice how some of the air threads peter out before reaching the base of the stem and that the air threads start in the solid base of the bowl. This latter feature shows it to be a two-piece glass.

43 *Centre:* An ale glass, *c.* 1760. The deep round funnel bowl is engraved with hops and (unusually) four ears of barley. There is a double-series air twist stem and a plain foot.

44 *Right:* A wine glass, *c.* 1760. It has an engraved drawn trumpet bowl, 'mercury' twist stem and a plain foot. This is in fact an air twist pattern, but its highly reflective nature explains the name of the stem.

stems are nearly always crisply moulded and the bowls are more in balance with the stems. On drinking glasses the style appears to have been in production for about twenty years before going out of fashion in the 1740's. Silesian stems did survive, however, on sweetmeat glasses, candlesticks and tazzas until the 1760's. I think that this was probably because these items had their counterparts in silver which continued to be made with Silesian style stems until late into the century.

Air twist stems

The idea of incorporating air into the stems of drinking glasses was not a new one. Glassmakers had long been aware of the fact that a bubble of air trapped in glass could be drawn out and elongated as the glass was manipulated. What was novel was the idea of arranging a series of air bubbles so that the elongation produced a definite pattern. When this technique was first developed is uncertain, but it was certainly being practised during the first half of the eighteenth century. F. Buckley recorded a glass bearing the date 1737 and another glass which went through one of the London sale rooms in 1979 was dated 1742. This latter was of the conventional drawn trumpet bowl type, but it had a domed foot, which is unusual.

Although this method of decoration was known before 1750

it was not until after that date that changing fashion and a demand for something more decorative created a climate which led to its general adoption. The third quarter of the eighteenth century produced the highest standards of aesthetic taste and an increasingly affluent society was in a mood to patronise artists, designers and craftsmen. A reaction set in against the plainness of the 1740's and paved the way for rococo and chinoiserie. There was no going back to the elaborately knopped and heavy glasses of the early eighteenth century. The Excise Act with its inhibiting effect on size, and the new elegance, demanded something different. It was in this context that the air twist and opaque twist styles of glassmaking became universally popular and cut glass found a market in spite of its price.

The commonest pattern of air twist stem is that known as a multi-ply spiral, which is a circle of air threads drawn out and twisted so that it fills the stem. Less common are the double series patterns that usually consist of a central twisted column of air threads surrounded by two opposed spiral threads. The other type of air pattern is that generally called 'mercury' twist. This is invariably composed of two thick strands of air, having a rectangular cross-section, twisted into a tight cork-screw. This pattern has a highly reflective quality which gives the air threads a silvery metallic appearance, and hence their name.

Because the air bubbles from which air twist stems were produced had a finite volume, there was a limit to how far they could be drawn out without breaking up or disappearing. It is not uncommon to come across air twist wine glasses where one or more of the individual strands terminate before it reaches the foot of the glass. Most air twist glasses are two-piece glasses, so that the stem of each one is individually made. For three-piece glasses the stems were made in lengths and then cut to size. Because of the limitations already described these lengths were short compared to the lengths produced for the opaque twist glasses discussed in the next section.

Having referred to dated glasses in this section, it would be convenient at this point to discuss the dating of glass generally. Most collectable antiques are fairly accurately identifiable and dateable. Silver has its hallmarks, pottery and porcelain their factory marks and pattern numbers, clock makers are well researched, and so on. Glass, however, is anonymous stuff and although the periods covering the principal styles have been identified, the actual maker and date of manufacture can only rarely be determined. This is why dated pieces, or glasses carrying inscriptions relating to known events are so important. They give us reference points to which we can relate other similar glasses. For the same reason, registration marks are also useful (see p. 155).

Opaque twist stems

I use this term out of personal preference, although 'enamel twist' and 'cotton twist' are other terms that are equally popular. All these terms describe that large quantity of eighteenth-century glasses which have a pattern of twisted white threads running through the stem. In a sense this could be described as a reversion to Venetian glassmaking, since this method of glass decoration was a peculiarly Venetian invention of the sixteenth century. They incorporated these lacy white patterns into glass vessels of all types under the names 'latticinio' or 'vetro di trina'. The fact that opaque twist and air twist complemented each other so well brought the style to prominence.

45 Three opaque-twist wine glasses, all with plain feet, *c.* 1760. (Left) A 'Lynn' wine glass which has a round funnel bowl with the distinctive horizontal rings associated with its Kings Lynn origin. (Centre) A drawn trumpet bowl. (Right) A round funnel bowl with moulded flutes.

Although the general effect was the same as air twist, the method of producing it was quite different. In this case a series of white glass rods (called enamel) are set into a mould which is then filled with molten clear glass. When this is set the resultant block is removed from the mould and coated in clear

glass. It is this mass which is re-heated, drawn and twisted to produce the rods from which the stems of glasses will be cut. Apsley Pellatt in his book *Curiosities of Glassmaking* gives a detailed account of this process, stating that lengths of up to sixty or seventy feet could be drawn.

Since the process was one of assembly rather than manipulation it meant that much more elaborate patterns could be achieved than was the case with air twist stems; limited only by the ingenuity of the glassmaker. Some collectors spend their time searching for as many variations of these stems as possible.

In addition to the white rods used to create these patterns coloured rods were sometimes used. These produced what are usually referred to as 'colour twist' glasses. The usual colours were red, blue, green and yellow, in descending order of frequency. Occasionally glasses appear with several colours in the stem, and these are called 'tartan' twist. Technically I can see no reason why it should be more difficult to include coloured threads among the white ones, but the fact remains that colour twist wine glasses account for a very small percentage of those that have survived. Perhaps they were not popular with the customer.

Opaque twist glasses are usually classified as having single, double or triple series twists. Where there is only one strand of enamel running through the stem this is clearly single series, but it is also possible to have a pattern consisting of a number of threads which is still single series. The criterion is that all the threads should form part of one distinct pattern. When a central pattern of one style, say a straight multi-strand tube, is surrounded by a spiral consisting of a series of threads in parallel, this is clearly double series. Three separate and distinct patterns gives a triple series twist, but this is extremely rare.

The English style of opaque twist and colour twist glasses was much copied on the Continent towards the end of the eighteenth century but they are fairly easy to distinguish, since they are made of soda glass, the bowl shapes are slightly different and the threads of colour are translucent. Bell bowls are narrower and flare more at the rim. Round funnel bowls have more parallel sides and are fuller in the base than English ones.

Although F. Buckley reported an opaque twist glass with a date as early as 1747 the bulk of these date from after 1750 and were contemporary with the air twist types. In 1777 another Excise Act doubled the duty on flint glass and introduced a new tax of 18/8d (93p) per cwt. on enamel glass. This must

46, 47 Two wine glasses, *c*. 1760. (Top) This bucket bowl, opaque-twist air stem with two spiral gauzes and plain foot is an unusual combination. (Above) A double ogee, or pan-top, bowl with faint vertical moulded flutes, a centre-knopped opaque-twist stem and a plain foot.

48 *Top:* A close-up view of
an incised-twist air stem.

49 *Above:* A wine glass,
c. 1750. The round funnel
bowl is dimpled at the base;
there is an incised-twist stem
and a plain foot.

have had a harmful effect on the trade in opaque twist glasses
anyway, but it also coincided with another major change of
style which put them quite out of favour. This was the
introduction of cut or facet stem glasses.

Before going on to look at these in detail, there are three
variations of the opaque twist/air twist period to consider.

Incised twist stems

For a short period in the middle of the eighteenth century,
about 1750 to 1765, glasses were made with finely ribbed and
twisted stems, and these are called incised twist. There are
amongst them some well-made lead glass examples, but the
majority are of indifferent quality, many of them being made of
soda glass. They were fairly easy to make and it is likely that
they were made as a cheap imitation of air twist glasses, as from
a distance the appearance is similar. Many of the lead metal
incised twist glasses have tapering, round funnel bowls which
are distinctly dimple moulded at the base. This suggests to me a
common origin and that they all originated from one glasshouse.

Mixed twist stems

As the name suggests, these are glasses which contain both air
and opaque threads. Mostly these are white threads, but a few
have survived with air threads in conjunction with colour or
white and colour threads. The distinguishing characteristic of a
mixed twist glass is that the two elements of the pattern should
be distinctly separate. Either a central air pattern surrounded
by a different pattern of opaque threads, or the reverse of this
is a true mixed twist. I make this point because I occasionally
have glasses represented to me as mixed twist when a single
insubstantial thread of air follows closely the line of one of the
strands of the opaque twist pattern. This, I am sure, was
unintentional and was an accident of manufacture.

Churchill's Glass Notes published annually between 1946
and 1956, gave comprehensive check lists of different types of
glass and the rarity of mixed twists is demonstrated by the fact
that of all the glasses in the air/opaque categories which are
recorded, the mixed twist ones account for only 3·2%.

Composite stems

A composite stem glass may be described as one which has a
stem containing sections of more than one recognisable style.
The majority have stems consisting of an air twist section and a
plain section, but opaque and plain sections are known. One

very rare glass has air and opaque sections separated by a central knop. When the air twist section is uppermost it usually runs into a large knop containing a ring of air beads before changing to a plain stem. They are usually quite striking glasses, but again from Churchill's check lists, account for only 6·5% of glasses with twist stems. It is not easy to determine whether they were made throughout the period of popularity of twist stem glasses or were confined to a few years during that period.

Facet stems

The last quarter of the eighteenth century saw the introduction of a totally new style of decoration, the cut or facet stem. For the whole of the eighteenth century the decorative aspect of drinking glasses had been incorporated during manufacture, either the external decoration produced by knops or the internal decoration of the air and opaque twist stems. Now, for the first time, the essential character of the glass was achieved by an applied technique.

Applied decorations such as engraving, gilding and enamelling had been practised at various times throughout the century, but they could be applied to any style of glass. With this last group, the decoration is the style.

Throughout the century cut glass had been made to serve a

50 *Left:* A mixed twist wine glass, *c.* 1760: round funnel bowl, stem with intertwined spiral gauze and a single opaque spiral thread, and plain foot.

51 *Centre:* A composite-stem wine glass, *c.* 1760: a thistle bowl with a solid base over a 'mercury' twist ending in a ball knop, a short air-beaded inverted baluster stem, a plain foot.

52 *Above:* A wine glass, *c.* 1790: a round bowl with everted rim and geometric cutting to the base, a stem cut with vertical flutes and a centre knop cut into diamonds, a plain foot cut into facets and with a scalloped edge.

53 A set of six wine glasses, c. 1790. The round bowls are engraved with an 'egg and dart' border and fine floral sprays. There are diamond-facet cut stems and plain feet.

luxury market. During the early years before a native tradition for glass cutting had grown, craftsmen were imported from Germany. With the imposition of the Excise in 1745 the market for cut glass was limited to an area where price was of no consequence. Cutting meant thick glass, thick glass meant weight, and weight cost money. This is why such articles as were cut for most of the period were luxury articles such as might grace a rich man's house. Chandeliers, candelabra, sweetmeats, dessert services and so on.

Cut stems first make their appearance in any quantity during the 1770's. As we have shown with the air and opaque twists, the techniques were known long before they became universally popular, and I am sure that the same was true of facet stems. How much the Excise of 1777 destroyed the market for opaque twist stems and left the market open for the introduction of facet stems, or how much they were a reflection of changing taste we shall probably never know. Whatever the reason, facet stems became the most popular glasses of the late eighteenth century because with them everybody could afford to have cut glass on their tables at a reasonable price. Reasonable, because the item to be cut (a plain stemmed wine glass) was easy to produce, because it did not have to be made especially thick and heavy to take the decoration, because the cutting was repetitive and did not require very skilled labour,

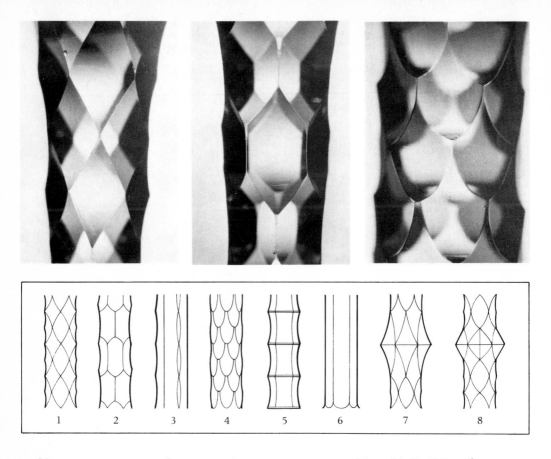

and because once mastered I am sure the operation was quickly carried out.

I have explained elsewhere in the book how the feet of drinking glasses developed during the century, and I sometimes come across plain stemmed wine glasses of a good clear metal with typically late eighteenth century feet that I am sure were meant to have cut stems but for some reason or another the operation was never carried out.

So much for the background; what of the cutting itself? There are two main types of facet cutting: diamonds and hexagons. Together they account for 80% of all cut stems. The pattern is achieved by first cutting the stem into a number of vertical flutes (six is the usual number) and then cutting a series of slices along each resulting edge, gradually cutting in deeper. The slices meet and the intersecting edges produce either diamonds or hexagons according to the length of the slice.

The remaining glasses in this group have a variety of patterns (see the diagram above) and it often surprises me that collectors do not show the interest in these variations that they show to unusual glasses of other styles. Apart from the

54, 55, 56 *Top:* Close-up views of: (Left) A diamond-facet stem. (Centre) A hexagon-facet stem. (Right) A scale, or shield, cut stem.

Above: **Facet cut stems.**
1 Diamond facets.
2 Hexagon facets.
3 Cut vertical flutes with alternate edges notched.
4 Scale or shield cutting.
5 Cut vertical flutes with band reliefs to produce narrow flat rings.
6 Cut plain vertical flutes.
7 Diamond facets with a central knop cut to plain straight edges.
8 Diamond facets with a swelling knop cut into pointed diamonds.

variations in cutting, the number of sides to the stem can also vary from four to eight. The greater the number of vertical flutes into which the stem is cut, the smaller are the resultant facets.

These glasses also occur with knops in the stems, and this feature also gives rise to variations in cutting. The cutting on the stem is usually carried over onto the base of the bowl and this is called bridge fluting or cutting. A further decorative feature commonly found on cut stem glasses is a band of small round polished circles alternating with crossed lines around the rim of the bowl. This is generally referred to as an 'egg and dart' or OXO border.

One final point of interest about this group is that one occasionally comes across an example with features that are out of character with the period; a folded foot, a domed foot or a drawn trumpet bowl are examples. All these features are more typical of glasses of the mid-eighteenth century and that, I am sure, is what they are. Remember that a facet cut stem starts out as a plain round stem. I think that when these cut stems became popular, people with glasses which were already thirty or forty years old sent them to be 'modernised'. The alternative to this is that these glasses were made with faceted stems in the mid-eighteenth century. If this were the case I would expect to come across far more of them than the two or three which I have seen over a period of many years. If one accepts that they were altered some years after they were made, and given the average collector's reluctance to buy pieces which have had later alterations made to them, should they be considered as desirable as facet cut glasses which are true to their period? I do not consider these as copies meant to deceive, but rather an expression of a domestic custom of the period and they are therefore worthy of attention now.

These glasses constitute the last group of typically eighteenth-century glasses; small bowls on tall stems and wide feet. By 1800 a totally new approach to style was making itself felt.

The glasshouses and glassmakers of the eighteenth century

So far this chapter has dealt only with the product of the eighteenth century and not with the industry itself. This is in contrast to the first chapter which dealt mainly with the developing glass industry. The reason, of course, is that little of the product of those early years has survived but the changing nature and the development of the industry is interesting

57 An example of what I am sure is an earlier glass cut later. A domed foot in conjunction with a drawn trumpet bowl and plain stem would have been uncommon in 1750 but non-existent in 1780, when I think the cutting was done. Had the cutting taken place in 1750 I should expect to find more glasses of that period with cut stems.

because it laid the foundations for the explosion in production during the eighteenth century. That explosion was due to the fact that the glass trade settled down into an orderly and well regulated industry lacking in the drama and excitement of earlier years. In a sense it had got over its growing pains, had settled down and become respectable.

In 1696 Houghton listed eighty-eight glasshouses in England and Wales, of which forty were making bottles and twenty-seven were making flint glass. Of the eighty-eight there were twenty-four in London, nine in the Bristol area, seventeen at Stourbridge and eleven in Newcastle-on-Tyne. Thus these four areas then accounted for 70% of glasshouses known to be working just before the start of the eighteenth century.

During the eighteenth century there are records of twenty-five glasshouses working in London, fifteen in Bristol, fourteen in Stourbridge and sixteen in Newcastle. By the time of the Excise Commission investigation in 1833 these figures had altered to four in London, four in Bristol, seventeen in Stourbridge and thirty-eight in Newcastle. It can be seen from these figures that by the end of the Georgian period glass-making had centred on Newcastle and Stourbridge. Today glassmaking has entirely disappeared from London and Bristol. Some industrial and utilitarian glassmaking survives in the Newcastle area and Stourbridge is the last of the great glassmaking districts still producing good quality domestic flint glass.

I am sometimes asked what antique glassware cost when it was new. This is an interesting question because if one knows what an article costs in relation to earnings when it was made, it is possible to draw conclusions as to what sort of market the object was made for and what class of people were likely to own it.

There are more records surviving today of glass prices during the late seventeenth century and early nineteenth century than there are for the collectable items of the eighteenth century. The main problem, though, is to know exactly what glasses are being referred to. Catalogues giving descriptions and prices before 1800 are virtually non-existent. Our main source of information is from surviving bills and invoices. These seldom list anything other than the mere shape or use of the glass.

The two most complete sources for seventeenth century glass are the list of prices agreed between Ravenscroft and the Glass Sellers Company and the Woburn Abbey invoices for glass supplied to the Duke of Bedford. From these it is possible to show that glassware was generally a rich man's luxury.

In the Ravenscroft/Glass Sellers price list of 29 May 1677 the prices were fixed by the weight of the glasses. Beer glasses, ribbed and plain, weighed 7 oz. and were 1/6d each, white beer glasses, nipped diamone waies, weighed 8 oz. and were 1/8d each. Claret glasses of the same two types weighed 5 oz. and $5\frac{1}{2}$ oz. and were 1/- and 1/3d each. These, of course, were prices to the Glass Sellers. The retail prices were higher, and it is interesting to see if any relationship can be made between these prices and those invoiced by the Glass Sellers to Woburn Abbey.

On 23 June 1676 we find twelve new flint wine glasses marked at 16/- but by August 1690 one dozen 'double flint' wine glasses were only 6/-. It is impossible to tell whether these were different types of glasses or similar but at much lower prices. It is perhaps reasonable to assume that during the life of Ravenscroft's patent his was the only source of supply of lead glass, so prices could be controlled. By 1690, however, the use of lead glass was widespread, competition was fierce and prices could have fallen considerably. So many of the Woburn invoices just refer to glasses without specifying exactly what they were. As a guideline, here are some typical examples of contemporary wages: In 1736 craftsmen such as carpenters and stone masons earned 7/- to 8/- per week. An estate bailiff living in earned £4.10.0 a year and a labourer 8 pence a day. In 1770 a weaver earned 8 shillings a week and miners fifteen shillings a week. By contrast professional men earned from £500 up-wards. When we compare these figures against the cost of glass in the eighteenth century we can gain some idea of the market which the glassmakers catered for.

Examples of prices charged during the eighteenth century come from a number of surviving invoices. For example, according to the accounts of Thomas Betts, a glass seller, in 1747 a dozen air twist wine glasses cost 6/- (30p) and in 1755 a dozen air twist champagne glasses with moulded bowls cost 10/6d (52½p) and six opaque twist wine glasses cost 6/- (30p). In 1773 Coleburn Hancock of Cockspur Street, Charing Cross supplied to Edward Gibbon: three pairs of quart decanters without stoppers at 12/-; two dozen wine glasses at 10/-; a dozen champagne flutes at 8/-; six half pint goblets at 4/6d. In 1791 tumblers sold at 6/- a dozen, and Rodney decanters at 6/- each. Some prices for Irish glass quoted by Westropp include two decanters for 5/8d in 1816, three pairs of salt cellars for 15/- in 1827 and best rummers at 8/6d a dozen in 1835.

If one can translate these sums into today's prices at current wage rates, wine glasses in the 1750's at 6d each (2½p) equals half to three-quarters of a day's wage for a working man, that is, about £8 to £12 today. A tumbler in 1790 at 8d equals £12 to £16 today. A Rodney decanter at 6/- would be £80 to £90 today, a figure which agrees very closely with the price of good quality modern cut lead crystal decanters these days.

For domestic use glass was undoubtedly confined to the middle and upper classes. What is less certain is how far it was in common use in inns and taverns. Then, as now, I imagine that when glass was used in such public places the quality would generally be inferior to that used domestically and the wastage rate was almost certainly much higher.

While lead glass reigned supreme, glass vessels were still being made from soda glass. These were generally more crudely made and were undoubtedly for a cheaper market. Given the wastage rate and the fact that soda was more brittle than lead glass, comparatively few have survived.

58 A goblet on a cut glass stem, *c.* 1740. It has been wheel-engraved with the motto of the Walpole family: *'Fari quae Sentio* Prosperity to Houghton'. Museum of London.

Cut glass

There is a fairly widespread popular belief which equates all cut glass with Ireland and then, by association, with Waterford. While Irish glassmaking undoubtedly became famous for its cut glass, the art was exported there from England, where it had been developed throughout the eighteenth century. Before going on to examine the Irish glass trade in more detail, let us consider the development of glass cutting in England.

As we have already seen, glassmaking in England derived from the Venetian tradition which was built around elaborate, thinly blown glass. This was not a product which was suitable for cutting, indeed even engraving on Venetian glass is unusual. This meant that when lead glass was developed there existed no native tradition of cutting except the bevelling and polishing of mirror plates, to exploit the possibilities of this new material. The softness of the metal, the increasing thickness of the sections it was possible to produce while preserving its clarity, and the lustre with which it reflected light were all qualities which made it ideal for cutting, and it is to the credit of the English glass trade that it realised the possibilities of this new method of decoration.

In Northern Europe, on the other hand, the Bohemian glassmakers had developed, during the seventeenth century, a hard white soda lime glass, which also lent itself to engraving and cutting, so by the time lead glass was making an impact on the English market the German cutters and decorators were already highly skilled in the art. It was to these craftsmen that

68

59 A sweetmeat glass, *c*. 1780. The ogee bowl has a cut everted rim and geometric cutting; the knopped stem is scale cut; the domed and cut foot has a scalloped rim.

the English glass trade turned, and the first cutters we hear of by name were Germans, and the earliest datable examples of English cut glass are very much in the German manner – baluster stem glasses with faceted knops. Before we learn of anyone cutting glass in this country the *London Gazette* in 1709 advertised a parcel of 'German cut and carved glass'. Then John Akerman, who was most probably German, comes to our notice in 1719 with an advertisement in the *Whitehall Evening Post* which said that he 'continues to sell . . . plain and diamond cut flint glasses'. He became a member of the Glass Sellers Company and was Master of that company in 1741. This illustrates the fact that the decoration of glass – engraving, cutting, enamelling, etc. – was related to the retail side of the trade rather than the manufacturing side. The work was done either in independent decorating workshops or by craftsmen employed by the Glass Sellers.

After this, Thomas Betts, whose trade card survives, had a shop in Pall Mall in about 1738 and Jerome Johnson, who advertised from 1739 to 1752, were only two of the many retailers selling all manner of objects in cut glass. Lustres, bowls, plates, dishes, mugs, bottles, cruets, decanters, salts, globes for lamps, salvers, even hookah bases for export.

During this period, from the introduction of German craftsmen up to the time of the 1745 Excise duty, the trade in cut glass expanded so that native English craftsmen were introduced to the art in the same way that they had been

60 A cut glass water jug, *c*. 1835. The shoulders are cut with short vertical panels between bands of prismatic cutting. The body is cut with alternate panels of fine diamonds and printies and gothic arches cut with larger pointed diamonds. The base is star cut.

61 *Above:* A canoe-shape bowl, *c.* 1820: scalloped rim with fan-and-husk cutting to the bowl, plain stem on a large square moulded foot ('lemon squeezer' foot).

62 *Left:* An unusual pair of cut candlesticks in the Adam style of 1780, but I believe these were made in the early nineteenth century.

63 A cut glass covered butter dish with stand, *c.* 1830.

brought into the glassmaking business during the years of Mansell's monopoly over a hundred years earlier. In the same way also this infusion of new blood and the requirements of English taste produced new styles of cutting which were distinctively different from their German origins.

With the imposition of the excise duty in 1745 and the consequent increase in the cost of raw material for cut glass wares, the market was severely inhibited, as explained on page 63. This led to a period of stagnation in design when the only part of the cut glass trade which flourished was that which supplied a market where price was no object. It is interesting to note that during the period from 1745 to the rise of the Irish Trade in the 1780's many of the surviving advertisements for sales of cut glass are those of retailers going bankrupt.

It was not until 1835 when the Glass Excise Tax was finally lifted that the cut glass trade really began to flourish in England, but as if it was a reaction against the restraints which had been imposed upon them for so many years, cutting was then practised to excess, with patterns becoming deeper and increasingly florid. Some of the examples of cut glass shown at the Great Exhibition of 1851, while demonstrating the highest degree of skill, exhibited a taste that was vulgar in the extreme. It was also incidentally the swan song of the Waterford Glass Company.

Because the styles of cutting, once developed, tended to change but little throughout the eighteenth century it is difficult to differentiate between early and late examples, and equally between English and Irish work. Generally, however, eighteenth century cutting tends to be shallow, or flat as it is sometimes described, which enables the glassmakers to keep the uncut weight to a minimum.

71

Chapter 3

Irish glass

There is a widespread popular belief that Irish glass has some quality not shared by glass made elsewhere in the British Isles. It is as if it arose complete and perfect like Venus from the waves to create a new standard of excellence. While this may seem a somewhat sweeping generalisation, I am intrigued by the considerable number of pieces of glass which are represented to me as being Irish and the frequency with which I am asked if pieces in my possession are Irish. The one thing they all have in common is that the pieces referred to are always cut glass. This highlights, perhaps, the most popular misconception of all. I hope during the course of this chapter to demonstrate that: *a* the widest variety of glassware was made in Ireland; and *b* that it was made there over a long period, usually by English glassmakers trying to escape political or economic restrictions in England but always working in the tradition in which they were raised.

The earliest records concerning the glass trade in Ireland go back to the middle of the thirteenth century, but until the late sixteenth century these more probably refer to glaziers rather than glassmakers, and if this is the case they would have imported their window glass from England. Both le Carré and Verzelini, when they obtained their licences, included the right to set up glasshouses in Ireland, but no evidence has come to light that they did so. It was more likely that they did this to protect themselves from unlicensed glassmakers setting up businesses in Ireland and evading the terms of their monopolies.

The first real evidence of a glasshouse working in Ireland dates to some time immediately prior to 1589. In that year the State papers of Ireland record the granting of a licence to run for eight years to Captain Thomas Woodhouse. The Patent Rolls of 1588 record that he had 'lately erected certain glass houses for making glass for glazing and drinking'. Woodhouse sold this licence to an Englishman, George Longe who in an effort to establish glassmaking in Ireland, introduced a Bill into

64 A peculiarly Irish vessel called a 'piggin', distinguished by its single handle. It is cut with alternate plain and diamond panels. The piggin derives from a wooden dairy vessel of the same name which was made of short barrel staves with one stave longer than the others to act as a handle. Glass copies such as this piece, *c*. 1830, were used as receptacles for milk or cream at table.

Parliament asking for the suppression of glasshouses in England and the transfer of the industry to Ireland, his argument being that such a course would preserve English woodland, exploit the abundance of wood in Ireland and provide employment for Irish workmen. Needless to say, such a grandiose scheme was contrary to the interests of both the English landowners and the glassmakers in England and so it failed, but there is evidence that a glasshouse existed for some years at this period near Curryglen in County Cork.

Subsequently several more patents were obtained for glass-making in Ireland, including one by Sir Robert Aston in 1606, but none of these schemes resulted in any progress being made towards developing an Irish industry. However, in 1611 William Robson, who had bought Sir Jerome Bowes' patent in England, also bought Aston's patent. These two patents gave him effective control over all glassmaking in Ireland, and in anticipation of the introduction of the coal fired furnace he set up a window glass factory in Ireland which, until it closed in 1618, sent considerable quantities of window glass to England.

It is possible that there were other glasshouses working in Ireland in 1613 because a letter from the Privy Council to the Lord Deputy for Ireland reminds him that there are patents in force covering glassmaking in Ireland and that all glasshouses not covered by these patents should be destroyed.

65 A large bucket-bowl rummer cut with the pillar-and-arch decoration found on a number of marked Waterford decanters, c. 1830.

The closure of William Robson's glasshouse appears to have resulted from the action taken by Sir Robert Mansell in 1616 to prevent the import of foreign glass (including Irish) into England in order to protect his own patents. Without this export market the glasshouse was uneconomic. This suggests that there was not sufficient demand in Ireland at that time to maintain a domestic source of supply.

There are subsequent records of glasshouses in 1618 at Ballynegery, County Waterford, and in 1623 at Birr in King's County. This latter was run by a member of the Bigo family, a descendant of the Lorraine De Bigaults who had settled on the Weald in the sixteenth century. The Bigo's were still operating glasshouses there in 1660. Boak's *Ireland's Natural History* records that this glasshouse made drinking glasses as well as window glass and that it imported sand from England. In 1670 Ananias Henzy, a descendant of the de Hennezells who had also helped to create the Wealden glass industry, started up a glasshouse at Portarlington in Queen's County.

In 1641 a Bill was passed prohibiting the use of wood in glasshouse furnaces, some twenty-five years after a similar one had been passed in England. Prior to this all the Irish glasshouses had been away from large towns, close to the woodlands, their source of fuel, but thereafter they moved into the coastal towns which gave easy access for the supply of fuel and raw materials: Dublin, Belfast, Waterford and Cork.

It can be seen from the foregoing that during the sixteenth and seventeenth centuries there was never sufficient domestic demand to support anything but the most meagre glass industry in Ireland; it was a poor country with very few people able to afford glazing for their windows or drinking glasses for their tables, and attempts to increase output by supplying the English market were at the mercy of the English monopolists.

From the end of the seventeenth century and during the first half of the eighteenth century glasshouses operated at Waterford and Dublin, but the Excise Act of 1745 not only created a burden for English glassmakers but dealt a death blow to the infant Irish industry. It provided that no glass could be exported from Ireland except on payment of ten shillings per pound duty and no glass could be imported into Ireland except that which was made in Great Britain. As a result of this, glassmaking was severely discouraged in Ireland, with glassmaking disappearing from Waterford and surviving only precariously in Dublin.

The glasshouse at Waterford had been established at a place called Gurteens just outside the town in about 1729, and advertised that it could supply 'all sorts of flint glass, double and single'. It also appears to have made all other types of glass, including bottles and window glass. It was advertised to let in 1740 but no other evidence suggests that it continued in operation.

Glassmaking in Dublin met with a little more success. There is evidence of glassmaking in the city from about 1677, but the most detailed evidence concerns a glasshouse set up in St. Mary's Lane about 1690 by a Captain Philip Roche. This survived as an operative glasshouse until about 1760 and it appears on Dublin maps subsequent to this date, but it was finally demolished in about 1787.

A number of advertisements in *Faulkner's Dublin Journal* spread over thirty-nine years from 1713 to 1752 give an insight into the enormous variety of glassware made in this glasshouse. There are only two references to cut glass: 'fine salts ground and polished' in 1729, but in 1752 they advertise 'all sorts of cut and flowered glass may be had of any kind to any pattern'. It is also interesting to note that in this last advertisement 'no pains or expense have been spared by the proprietor to secure the best workmen and newest patterns from London'. This

66 An early eighteenth-century goblet commemorating the Battle of the Boyne, 1690. It shows William III with cavalry and infantry crossing the River Boyne.

suggests that the wealthier members of Irish society looked to London as the source of fashion and quality.

Another Dublin flint glasshouse opened about 1734 in Fleet Street, which advertised of its wares 'workmanship equal to those made in London'. It appears to have burned down in 1741. A further bottle and window glasshouse operated in Batchelors Walk from 1725 to the 1740's. Other bottle glass-houses operated from about 1750 onwards, and again in 1754 the Dublin Journal stated that 'Mr. William Gordon (had) just brought over from England a complete set of as good workmen as any in the country, for the new glasshouse at the Ship Buildings'.

In 1759, three Englishmen, Jeudwin, Landon and Lunn, took over the Abbey Street glasshouse to make window glass, and stated before the Dublin Society in 1762 that they employed sixty workmen, of whom fifty were Englishmen. In 1768 they gave evidence before the Irish Parliament that they had instructed Irish hands and trained Irish apprentices but that the foreign artists (English) refused to work with the Irish. (Shades of le Carré's problems with the Lorraine glassmakers in the 1560's.)

The third important flint glasshouse to operate in Dublin was that of Richard Williams & Company. There were several members: Richard William, Thomas and Isaac. They came from England and appear to have taken over an existing bottle glass factory in Marlborough Green in 1764. From 1770 their advertisements offered a wide range of glassware 'equal to any imported in quality of metal and workmanship', and in 1774 they offered glass lustres, girandoles and chandeliers. These are essentially cut glass items for a luxury market. This firm, then, was well established by the time the export restrictions were lifted in 1780 and in a good position to take advantage of the new opportunities about to be offered.

There were several window and bottle glasshouses working during this period, but it is clear that English workmen and English taste played an important role in the manufacture of glass during those years.

We now come to the period which allowed Irish glassmaking to expand and develop a product that has impressed itself on our consciousness down to the present day. The events which triggered off this dramatic change were the doubling of the duty in 1777 on glass made in England and, more importantly, the Act of 1780 which exempted the Irish glass trade from the duty and removed the restrictions on exporting glass. Another Act of 1781 lifting the duty on imported coal used in

67 *Far left:* Irish decanter, *c.* 1800, marked on the base 'B. Edwards'. There are three feathered neck rings and moulded flutes to the base. This latter feature is common among Irish decanters.

68 *Left:* Although this decanter is similar in style, it is marked on the underside 'Cork Glass Co.', *c.* 1800.

glassmaking also contributed to the economic advantages of making glass in Ireland. Within three or four years glasshouses were operating in Dublin, Belfast, Cork, Waterford and Newry. The many surviving records and advertisements for these glasshouses show that they made all types of glassware, but cut glass accounted for an ever-increasing amount of the output. The glassmakers must have realised that the prohibitive duty on cut glass in England gave them a greater advantage in that field than in the plainer glass. This price advantage probably meant that much more cut glass was exported than the other types and thus, outside Ireland, Irish glass would have become synonymous with cut glass. Before going on to examine the product and the styles, let us have a look at these glasshouses in the years following the 1780 Act.

Dublin

The Williams family business appears to have been variously under the direction of its several members until 1827 when it closed, but during its life it was the most important glasshouse in Dublin. Other firms who operated there were Charles Mulvaney from 1785-1846 and Thomas and John Chebsey from 1786-98. Another business started as J. D. Ayckbown & Co. about 1799 and closed as J. Jynn Rogers & Co. about 1808. Ayckbown came from England where he had been a member of a glassmaking family who had probably originally come from Germany as glass cutters in the early years of the eighteenth century. The only other important glasshouse to operate in

Dublin was that of Thomas & John Pugh, which started in 1852 and ran until 1895 when Westropp says that the manufacture of flint glass ceased in Ireland.

One of the problems in tracing the history of glasshouses is the frequent changes of ownership they seemed to enjoy. Partners came and went and bankruptcies were not uncommon.

Belfast

Glassmaking in Belfast centres around Benjamin Edwards, an English glassmaker from Bristol. In 1771 the owners of the Tyrone Collieries decided to set up a glasshouse since there were readily available supplies of the necessary raw materials: coal, sand and clay. Edwards went to Ireland to initiate this enterprise at Drumrea near Dungannon, but it seems to have survived for only a very few years, since in 1776 he set up a glasshouse in Belfast where he advertised all kinds of glassware for sale. One of the advertisements states that he had brought a glass cutter from England. Edwards had three sons, and until Benjamin Snr. died in 1812 the management of the business changed frequently amongst them. After this the company was run by Benjamin Jnr. until 1827.

One of the sons, John, set up his own glasshouse in 1803 but was not successful, and sold out in 1804. Various interests ran this as the Belfast Glass Works until 1840.

Cork

It was the practice of the Dublin Society to offer premiums, or subsidies, to encourage the setting up of business enterprises in Ireland in an effort to encourage trade. Cork, because of its good natural harbour and trade links with the rest of the world, was an ideal centre for this, and the Dublin Society had offered premiums for the erection of a glasshouse there in 1753. It was not until 1783, however, after the granting of free trade, that Hayes, Barnett and Rowe petitioned Parliament for aid in introducing the glass trade to Cork. They had sent to England to obtain the best equipment, materials and workmen available and had established two glasshouses, one for bottle glass, the other for flint.

This was the origin of the Cork Glass Company which ran until 1818. During that period there was a succession of partners and changes of ownership but, after Waterford, the Cork glasshouses are the best known and remembered. In 1815, towards the end of the life of the Cork Glass Company, Daniel Foley set up a new glasshouse on Wandesford Quay. This was the Waterloo Glass Company and again it survived various bankruptcies and changes of ownership until 1835. Its demise was largely due to the effects of the Excise Duty imposed on Irish glass in 1825. (We know this from notices in Cork newspapers advertising the auction sale of equipment of the glasshouse at Wandesford Quay to recover unpaid excise duty.) In competition with it for most of its life was the Terrace Glass Works, started by brothers Edward and Richard Ronayne in 1818 and surviving until 1841.

I think that the reason the Cork Glass Company and the Waterloo Glass Company are so much better known than the last mentioned is that glassware marked with the names of both these companies has survived, while I know of no marked piece of Terrace Glass Works glass.

Waterford

As mentioned earlier, there was no glassmaking in Waterford after 1740 until 1783. In that year brothers George and William Penrose, merchants in Waterford, realising the advantages offered to them by the Act of 1780, established the Waterford Glass Company. This was to become the most famous of all the Irish glasshouses, and is even today credited with most of the cut glass made during the nineteenth century.

The Penrose brothers were not glassmakers themselves, so they had to import the expertise they required. Thus the Waterford glasshouse was started up by John Hill of Stourbridge, who took with him a sufficient number of glassmakers to carry out all the functions of a glasshouse.

After three years in charge of the glasshouse, Hill was accused (we don't know whether justly or unjustly) of some indiscretion by the wife of one of the Penroses. This resulted in him leaving Waterford for France, but before leaving he entrusted his glassmaking recipes to Jonathan Gatchell, a clerk at the glasshouse, with whom he had become friendly. The mixing of the batches of the raw materials was most important, for on this rested the quality of the glass. Presumably it was also fairly secret because it made Gatchell a most important man in the glasshouse. He went on to learn the whole glassmaking business, and some time after William Penrose's death in 1796 he bought out the remaining brother in 1799, going into partnership with James Ramsey and Ambrose Bancroft, these two putting up the capital while Gatchell supplied the expertise. However, Ramsey died in about 1811 and Gatchell then bought out Bancroft and became the sole owner. The Waterford Glass Co. remained with descendants of the Gatchell family until it finally closed in 1851 after having exhibited at the Great Exhibition. No glass was then made in Waterford until a new company started up in business as Waterford Glass Ltd. in 1951.

The vogue for cut glass carried on well into the second half of the nineteenth century and much of the glass I see represented as Waterford falls into that period when there was no glasshouse working there.

One other point I must emphasise, although many writers have already dealt with the subject, is the question of colour in Waterford glass. Hartshorne in his book *Antique Drinking Glasses* of 1896, attributed a blue colour to Waterford glass, and although so many writers have since tried to dispel this mistake I find that it is still a widespread belief. Westropp in 1920 wrote that none of the examples of Waterford glass in his possession showed a blue tint, and in a catalogue to accompany an exhibition of Waterford glass at Waterford in 1952, it is stated that 'Waterford glass has many . . . qualities, but a bluish colour is not amongst them'. The colour in old glass is accidental, depending on the presence of impurities in the silica. Old records show that much of the sand used at Waterford was shipped from the Isle of Wight and Kings Lynn, with the Lynn sand being considered the better.

During the years from 1780 to 1825 the Irish glass trade flourished. England had always been looked to as the source of style and fashion, and during much of the eighteenth century Englishmen had set up glasshouses in Ireland and English glass craftsmen had found employment there. This trend accelerated after the granting of free trade, and there are many reports of English operatives working in Ireland. There are those who argue that a distinctive Irish style arose out of this upsurge in trade, and from marked pieces of Irish glass it is possible to identify recurring patterns which can sometimes lead to a reasonable attribution to a particular glasshouse, but these spring from the preference of the management or the cutters and were not exhibitions of a uniquely Irish style. The English craftsmen must have taken with them the tradition in which they were trained, and would continue to make styles which were equally popular in England at the same time.

Much has been made of the pages of designs left by Samuel Miller, foreman cutter of Waterford, of patterns used in the 1830's and 1840's. There is no evidence to suggest that they all originated in Waterford, and many decanters turn up in England today which conform to some of these patterns. Numerous records have survived of Irish glass exports covering the years 1781 to 1822 and the only town which appears to have exported to England was Cork, otherwise the principal markets for these Irish exports were the West Indies and North America, with some being sent to Italy, Spain and Denmark.

In the Waterford records there are several references of attempts to export to England. About one such venture in 1832 Jonathan Wright and George Saunders took a consignment to Southampton to sell by auction. Many people looked at the goods but would not buy and some, on learning they were Irish said they could not be any good. The reputation of Waterford was apparently not as strong then as now! But in Exeter in 1832 Elizabeth Walpole, another partner in the firm, persuaded a local retailer to stock Waterford glass, which he apparently found acceptable.

In 1825 the Irish glass trade was subjected to Excise Duty. This was calculated on a complicated basis relative to the weight of glass metal in the glass pots and the finished weight of goods manufactured. Some relief was granted for exported glassware. The collection of this duty was strictly supervised with Excise Officers being stationed in each glasshouse and having absolute control over the mixing, loading and firing of the raw materials. They controlled access to the glass pots and the amount of metal taken from them. In fact the whole operation of the glasshouse was at the mercy of these Excise Officers. During the first year of its operation the Waterford Glass Company paid £3910.7s.5d. in duty.

It is not surprising that from this time Irish glassmaking started to decline. It had lost its competitive advantage over English glass and the liberty of the glassmakers was inhibited by bureaucracy. From a high point in 1825, when there were eleven glasshouses working in Ireland, by 1852 there were only three. What finally put paid to the industry in Ireland was the lifting of all Excise Duty on the industry throughout the United Kingdom in 1845. Ireland could not then hope to compete with glass made in England and Scotland, and had to be content with satisfying the small domestic market.

Products and identifying characteristics

After this review of the Irish glassmaking industry, what of the products it made? The following is a list of some of the articles named in advertisements appearing in Irish journals from 1729 onwards.

1729 Salvers, baskets with handles and feet for desserts, salts, decanters, lamps.

1749 Fine large globe lamps for one to four candles. Bells and shades, sweetmeat and jelly glasses, glasses for apothecaries, water glasses, jugs, orange glasses, covers for tarts.

1752 Claret and Burgundy bottles, saucers, sillabub glasses, sucking bottles, cupping glasses, funnels. All sorts of glass for electrical experiments. Wine glasses with a vine border, toasts or any flourish whatever, beer ditto; tea canisters, mustard pots.

1816 Goblets, tumblers, ladles, salad bowls.

1823 Ringed decanters, footed salts.

1842 Chandeliers, lustres, hall bells, candelabra.

1849 Liqueur bottles, carafes, pickle urns, claret jugs, celery vases, sugar bowls, butter coolers, cream ewers.

Many of these appear in more than one advertisement, of course, but it does give some idea of the tremendous variety of glassware available during the eighteenth and nineteenth centuries.

It has never been easy to discriminate between English and Irish glass made prior to 1780. There are a number of glasses which bear engraving relating to Irish organisations or events. These are identical with English glasses of the period, and if they were in fact made in Ireland, they emphasise the similarity between the two manufactures. There is one type of glass, however, which is normally given an Irish attribution and this is a cordial glass with a small bowl, an unusually thick, tall plain stem and usually a domed foot.

We then enter a period, from 1780, when it is easier to relate pieces to particular factories. The bulk of attributed or proven glass was made after that date, and most of it is cut to some degree. Fortunately, several of the Irish glasshouses adopted a method of making certain items which, when taken in conjunction with the styles of decoration, enables us to make reasonable attribution of unmarked items. The method used was to blow flat-bottomed pieces such as decanters and finger bowls into open moulds, which had the glass company's name incorporated into them. Pieces marked with the names Cork Glass Co., Waterloo Co., Cork, Penrose, Waterford, and B. Edwards may be found. There are other names marked on pieces of Irish glass, but they are for retailers rather than manufacturers. Among these are Francis Collins, Dublin; J. D. Ayckbown, Dublin; Armstrong, Ormond Quay (Dublin); C. M. & Co. (for Charles Mulvaney).

Associated with the name moulded into the base is usually a ring of fine vertical moulded flutes around the lower half of the vessel. On decanters particular types and numbers of neck rings are associated with particular factories. These are the distinguishing marks which are incorporated at the time of manufacture. The cutting is applied afterwards and can, of course, vary enormously, but particular patterns turn up frequently enough to allow reasonable attributions to be made on unmarked pieces. Thus, the pillar and arch cutting and single rows of strawberry diamonds occur on Waterford pieces.

Engraved bows between cross-hatched loops and circles are typical of marked Waterloo pieces.

Looped vesica pattern with cross-hatching alternating with stars is a typical Cork Glass Company feature.

All Edward decanters have only two neck rings (but so does at least one Armstrong decanter).

Amongst table glass, the canoe bowl on moulded pedestal foot, the kettledrum bowl and bowl with turn-over rim are all shapes associated with Irish glassmaking.

These associations provide sufficient evidence, I think, to make reasonable attributions in unmarked pieces, but other than this I am sure there is much wishful thinking in adding the word Irish to examples of cut glass. That is not to say that there are not many examples of glassware made in Ireland surviving today. My point is that it is unwise to accept as Irish any piece of glass for which reasonable evidence is not forthcoming. If the item is attractive and well made in its own right, does the label Irish suddenly make it more desirable?

One last point which, if not realised, can only lead to more confusion is that skilled glassmakers and decorators were always in demand, and they often moved from one glasshouse to another, so very similar styles and patterns were executed in several glasshouses.

Before leaving the subject of Irish glass I must refer to that most Irish of all styles the Williamite glass. This is a style of engraved decoration which appears on a number of different types of drinking glass and takes its inspiration from the victory of William of Orange at the Battle of the Boyne, 1 July 1690. The earliest glass I know of with this engraving dates from about twenty-five years after the event and it then appears regularly on glasses made during the next 200 years. Many people refer to these as copies or fakes, but we have here an instance where a particular historical event became adopted as the symbol of a political idea. So when the inscription 'To the Glorious Memory of King William' or 'Battle of the Boyne, 1 July 1690' appears on a glass made in late Victorian times it is not a copy in the normal sense of the word, but the continuing expression of the political ideals of the Orange Order.

Types of cutting found on decanters.
1 Vertical panels. Used for base and shoulders.
2 Strawberry diamonds.
3 Crosscut relief diamonds.
4 Fine relief diamonds.
5 Pillar flutes.
6 Swags or drapery.
7 Bulls eye or lunar slices.
8 Flat hobnail diamonds.
9 Prismatic cutting.
10 Comb flutes.
11 Slanting blazes.

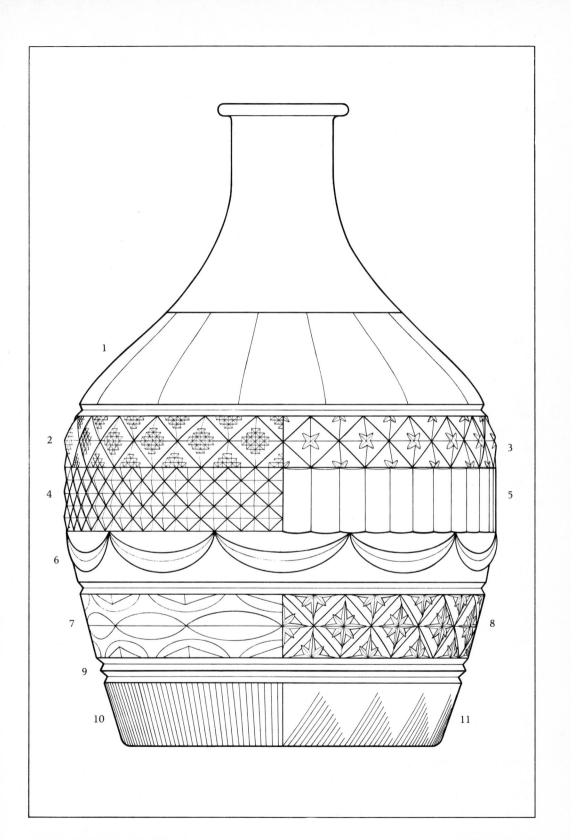

Chapter 4

Late Georgian glass

The published literature on glass deals exhaustively with the history and development of the glass trade up to about 1800. After that date most writers have concerned themselves either with late Georgian cut glass or Victorian coloured and decorative glass. Nineteenth century drinking glasses have not generally merited the attention which their increasing interest to collectors demands.

The last decade of the eighteenth century saw a change in taste away from the long-stemmed glasses which had dominated the market for so long, towards glasses on short or rudimentary stems. For the first time for over a century drinking glasses came into general use which had a capacity conforming more nearly to modern ideas. In contrast to these, an endless variety of small glasses was made for a market which had apparently tired of the stemmed glasses of the previous years.

It might be argued that this was a period of decline leading to a new departure in glassmaking, but this would belie the many variations that may still be found on a limited number of themes. They represent a rich source of material for the collector of modest means. They are generally very reasonably priced in comparison with the better-known glasses of the eighteenth century. They satisfy that widespread preference for collecting things which are 'Georgian' and they are sufficiently varied to enable an interesting collection to be built up. I have met many enthusiastic collectors who made their first acquaintance with antique glass through examples of this period and who, as their knowledge and confidence grew, graduated to collecting earlier specimens.

Rummers

Drinking glasses of the early 1800's fall generally into three categories: rummers, ale glasses and small glasses for wines or spirits. Rummers were the largest of these and their bowls, holding eight to ten fluid ounces, contrast sharply with the

69 A roemer not a rummer, c. 1820. It has a cup bowl surmounting a hollow stem decorated with an applied collar and prunts. The foot is conical with a trail of glass applied to the upper surface. In the continental originals the foot was made of a thread of glass wound around a cone.

two- to three-ounce capacity of the earlier glasses. The origin of the title 'rummer' to describe these glasses is obscure, but there are two main schools of thought. The first suggests that the word is a corruption of the German 'roemer'. This was a wine glass, popular in Northern Europe from the sixteenth century, which was used for Rhenish white wine. Its principal characteristics were that it had a large capacity round bowl on a wide hollow stem and a small conical foot made of a single thread of glass wound round a wooden cone. It may be seen represented in many Dutch and German still-life paintings of the seventeenth century. Rhenish wine has been drunk in Britain for centuries and this style of glass was well known. There is a design for such a glass among the patterns which Greene ordered from Morelli in Venice and a large example bearing the raven's head seal of Ravenscroft is in the Victoria and Albert Museum. Although the name and style does not appear to have been used during the eighteenth century there was a revival of interest in them in the early nineteenth century when an anglicised version was made in coloured glass in Britain. A pattern book of the Edinburgh & Leith Glass Company illustrates these glasses, calling them 'Romers' but they are of much smaller capacity than their Continental originals. The only connection I can make between these roemers and the British rummer is that they both have large bowls on short stems and feet smaller than the diameter of the bowl.

The other derivation of the name is linked to the increasing popularity of rum-based drinks during the later eighteenth century. Whereas neat spirits would only require small glasses,

70 Three rummers. (Left and right) A pair of round bowl rummers with square 'lemon squeezer' feet, *c*. 1820. (Centre) A rummer with a round bowl engraved with bows and festoons, *c*. 1800. There is a short plain stem and a folded foot, the latter is rare on rummers.

rum-based toddies, to which hot water was added, presumably required larger ones.

Whatever the reason, rummers made their appearance late in the eighteenth century and by the early years of the nineteenth century had become one of the most popular styles of drinking glass. As they came into more general use I am sure they were used for a wider variety of drinks; there are many engraved with hops and barley, denoting their use as ale glasses, and occasionally one may find one engraved with grapes and vine leaves, which suggests its use as a wine glass.

The earliest rummers had thinly blown round bowls with moulded panel decoration to the lower half, a short rather thin stem and a plain foot much smaller than the diameter of the bowl. A little later a collar or merese was introduced between the bowl and the stem, which then tended to be made somewhat thicker. As time went on new bowl shapes were introduced. It is hard to be precise about the order in which these were developed, but based on slight changes in quality and detail amongst those I have examined, my own opinion is that the sequence was probably: round bowl, ogee bowl, bucket bowl, double ogee bowl, barrel bowl. Whatever the order, all these shapes appeared during the first quarter of the nineteenth century. One feature which is noticeable is that as the century progressed the glass tended to get thicker, the quality of the metal improved, and more decoration was achieved by cutting. Ogee bowl rummers usually have thick plain stems while the others frequently have short stems with somewhat rudimentary knops, the earlier ones having blade knops while later on the ball knop was popular.

71 A bucket-bowl rummer engraved with a crest and monogram and the year 1826. There is a short knopped stem and a plain foot.

Ale glasses

Although many rummers were used as beer glasses, the ale glass proper had been a staple product of the glass trade from pre-Ravenscroft days. True ale glasses were distinguished by their narrow, deep bowls which are generally referred to as flutes. Greene ordered ale flutes from Morelli, but these were almost certainly much taller than those made by the English glassmakers. Ravenscroft supplied beer glasses to the Glass Sellers Company but it is not clear just what shape these were. By 1700, however, the style of ale glass which is familiar to all collectors of English glass had evolved. These typically had a narrow funnel bowl with wrythen or gadrooned decoration and often a flammiform fringe on a short stem. This was sometimes pincered into four or five wings beneath the bowl, to create the so-called propeller stem, and the folded foot. As

72 A panel-moulded rummer with an ovoid bowl engraved with festoons and stars. There is a short plain stem and plain foot, c. 1800.

73 Four ale glasses: (Left to right) Gadrooned wrythen bowl, plain stem, folded foot, c. 1690; Wrythen funnel bowl, propellor knopped stem, folded foot, c. 1700; Gadrooned wrythen bowl with a flammiform fringe, short plain stem, folded foot, c. 1720; Wrythen funnel bowl, short knopped stem, folded foot, c. 1730.

this style of ale glass continued to the 1730's it changed its character slightly. The gadrooning was not so heavy, the wrythen pattern became more precise and the stem was reduced to little more than one or two rudimentary knops between bowl and bowl and folded foot. I emphasise this because some authorities credit this type of ale glass to the late eighteenth century, but my own experience suggests that gadrooning on these glasses went out of fashion by the 1730's, never to return.

The standard bowl shape survived the decline of gadrooning, and it appears on all the different stem types of the eighteenth century from baluster stems to facet stems. Several of the well-known bowl shapes were elongated and modified to produce the typical ale glass style; round funnel, ogee and bell bowls among them. At the end of the century, as the short stemmed glasses found favour, the ale glass reverted to the proportions it had had at the beginning of the century but this time it had an entirely different character. The wrythen pattern was achieved by blowing the bowl into a conical mould which had vertical grooves. This produced a ribbed effect on the glass. If the bowl was twisted while the metal was still plastic the ribs were twisted and produced the typical wrythen pattern. The plasticity of the glass affected the amount of twist that could be imparted to it and so one rarely sees two wrythen ales of this period with exactly the same amount of twist. The stem is usually reduced to one or two ribbed knops with no

87

more than a token plain section, and the foot is a thick, plain, flat foot which is common around 1800. A variation on this is an ale having a short incised twist stem with the pattern running up into the lower part of the funnel bowl.

Other than these wrythen patterns there are many other patterns of ale glass covering the period 1800-40, plain bowls and stems, panel moulded bowls, knopped stems, plain and folded feet. Many of them are engraved with hops and barley denoting their use.

I have already mentioned that rummers became both thicker and heavier by the middle of the nineteenth century, and this is equally true of ale glasses. The dwarf ale flute of the early nineteenth century, which was about $5\frac{1}{2}$ inches high, gradually gave way to ale glasses which were about 7 inches high with parallel-sided, round-bottomed bowls on short, thick plain stems and wide feet. When these were decorated the most popular pattern was a series of round polished depressions called printies. These were in rows around the bowl and for most of its height.

74 Five ale glasses spanning the period 1720-1820: (Left to right) Knopped facet-stem ale glass, *c.* 1780; Dwarf ale glass engraved with hops and barley, *c.* 1820; Funnel bowl baluster-stemmed ale glass with an annulated knop, *c.* 1720; Facet-stemmed ale glass engraved with Masonic symbols, *c.* 1790; Plain-stemmed ale glass engraved with hops and barley, *c.* 1750.

Small glasses

As I mentioned at the beginning of this chapter, the wide variety of small glasses made during the late eighteenth and early nineteenth centuries have been neglected by earlier writers. Such was the variety of period glassware available before the last war that none of the standard works on the subject considered them worthy of any attention. Since then they have slowly received more recognition but I still meet many collectors who complain of a lack of information regarding the dating of these glasses.

First let us define them. What sets them apart from other small glasses of the eighteenth century? Until about 1780 small glasses which are generally referred to as spirit or dram glasses were scaled down versions of the standard wine glasses of the day. Thus we find the standard bowl shapes and sizes on short, thick, opaque twist and plain stems, usually in conjunction with a thick foot. From 1780 we find that they have been replaced by glasses which generally have funnel bowls on thin plain stems with plain or folded feet. They are seldom more than $4\frac{1}{2}$ inches high. The change, then, is not only one of style but also of weight and I think this is the key to their appearance. The doubling of the Excise Duty in 1777 with further increases in 1781 and 1787 put an enormous burden on the glassmakers. Much of the business must have been with innkeepers where spirits, mainly gin, were an important part of their trade. To satisfy this market, cheaper and therefore lighter glasses were necessary. Many of these glasses are engraved with decorated borders. The poor quality of this engraving also suggests they were made for a cheap market.

Slowly the use of these glasses became established and as it did so the variety of patterns increased. As new shapes of rummer made their appearance, so they were copied in smaller versions. Also, as their use extended they lost their connection with spirits and became accepted as wine glasses. By 1830 they had become standard domestic drinking glasses and continued so for about another twenty years. Those that follow the rummer shapes are easy to date, but by the 1830's they were beginning to develop a style that owed nothing to larger glasses. They have relatively deep, straight-sided bowls, rounded at the bottom. Panel moulding was common and many of them have an out-turned lip. The stems are decorated with small ball knops at the centre and the base or both and the feet are flat, somewhat roughly made and relatively thick.

One thing about glasses of this period which troubles many people is that they have folded feet. Popular opinion has it that a folded foot is a guarantee of an eighteenth century glass, but this is not so. There was a period between 1800 and 1830 when the folded foot was commonly used on many small glasses. I

75 *Above left:* Two small wine glasses, both with folded feet, *c.* 1820. (Left) An engraved bucket-bowl with a short knopped stem. (Right) An engraved and panel-moulded ogee bowl on a stem with ribbed knops.

76 *Above:* Two small wine glasses, *c.* 1850. Both have panel cutting to the bowl, knopped stems and plain feet.

77 *Left:* Two small wine glasses. (Left) Cut bucket-bowl, *c.* 1830. (Right) Plain bucket-bowl and a folded foot, *c.* 1820.

think this was partly weight-saving and partly because the lighter character of the folded foot was more in keeping with the glasses themselves. The thing to bear in mind is the style of the whole glass, particularly the bowl. Where rummer shapes are copied, that should establish the date with certainty.

The most popular of these rummer shapes translated to small glasses was the bucket bowl. It occurs on glasses of every quality from the plainest to the most elaborately cut versions which suggests that the popularity of these little glasses reached every level of society. The years between 1820 and 1830 saw the introduction of plain stems but with vertical flutes and it became more and more normal for the pontil mark to be polished out.

90

Extending into early Victorian times these glasses became even more sophisticated with cut panels replacing the moulded panels, and the simple knopping giving way to miniature versions of the early baluster stems, inverted and true balusters, blade, angular and dumbbell knops may all be found on these glasses. They survived as general purpose glasses until the later Victorian glassmakers introduced the idea of having suites of glasses with a different shape being made for each type of drink.

There is one very distinctive feature of this period which was so widely used on glass of all types that I feel it best to discuss it separately. This was the moulded pedestal base or foot. It is popularly known as the lemon squeezer foot, since most examples are ridged inside in the manner of old-fashioned lemon squeezers.

This type of base first made its appearance in the late eighteenth century but enjoyed its greatest success in the period up to 1830. Glassware incorporating this feature is made by two techniques: moulding and blowing. The method is ideal where short stems are used, since the foot and stem can be moulded as one unit and then fixed to the bowl. The technique was to squeeze the glass into a shaped mould using a punch which produced the plain or patterned recess in the base. The process could not have been exact since there was usually a surplus of glass which emerged to leave a ragged edge around the foot, and this had to be removed by grinding and polishing. While the majority of these feet are square, many other shapes were produced, diamonds and ovals for salt cellars, hexagons and octagons for ale glasses, and indented quatrefoil shapes for condiment bottles. Massive versions were produced for the canoe-shaped bowls associated with Irish glassmaking, and recently several salt cellars have come to my notice which have raised letters moulded on the upper surface. The letters are *P* and *H*, or *P*, *T* and *H*. The exact sequence is unknown, since nobody knows the starting point. Presumably these refer to the maker, but I have so far been unable to find the name of any glassmaking company whose name starts with these letters.

From dated examples I believe that the earliest square moulded feet had only a plain depression in the underside, the ribbed pattern making its appearance a little later. It was widely used on rummers, and some of the most pleasing ones have a straight-sided bucket bowl on a tall moulded base with the ribbed pattern deeply indented into the underside so that it shows through. The bowls are generally thinly blown and invariably of good quality. One feature like this can become the theme for an interesting collection. I am sure it would be difficult to exhaust all the possibilities of foot pattern and the vessels on which they are found.

Decanters

Although the majority of Georgian decanters which survive today date from the years after 1800, their history goes back to the late seventeenth century. Their original purpose was to replace wine bottles on the table, and some of the very earliest examples are no more than clear glass versions of contemporary green glass wine bottles. At that time wine bottles were of a squat onion shape with tapering necks. The clear or flint glass versions of these usually had longer, somewhat narrower, necks and are generally referred to as shaft and globe decanters. That some decoration was added to these is shown from a surviving price list of Ravenscroft which refers to quart, pint and half pint ribbed bottles and similar sizes 'nipt diamond waies', i.e. with a trailed diamond pattern all over them, which is referred to on p. 67.

By the early years of the eighteenth century the body of these serving bottles had been developed into hexagonal or octagonal shapes and they often had a loop handle added. However, it was not the practice to have fitted glass stoppers; the old practice of adding a string ring to the neck still survived. Before the advent of accurately cut corks and corking machines bottles were stopped with plugs of oiled hemp or tapering corks. These were held in place by a thread passed over the top and anchored to the string ring.

From about 1730 to 1750 a new shape appeared. This was the cruciform decanter, which in plan view looked like a very short-armed cross. These still retained the string ring, but it often consisted of a thread wound two or three times round the neck. Although it would not be normal practice to stopper these bottles, this multiple string ring provided a useful grip when using the bottle.

The essential thing about all these early styles was that they were purely serving bottles rather than storage bottles. The contents would be decanted from wine bottles or barrels and what was not drunk at table could presumably be returned to the storage vessel.

It is not until about 1760 that the first bottles appear which we would term decanters today. These were more elegant containers with slightly tapering cylindrical bodies with shoulders which curved inward to a short parallel neck. These dispensed with the string or neck ring, and for the first time

78-82 These decanters were all made between 1790 and 1860.
Above: A mallet-shape decanter with facet-cut neck and stars to the body, *c.* 1790. *Opposite above left:* An elaborately cut decanter, *c.* 1820. *Opposite above right:* A decanter cut with diamond columns and gothic arches, *c.* 1840. *Opposite below left:* A Prussian-style decanter which has three triple neck rings, *c.* 1830. *Opposite below right:* A straight-sided decanter with its body divided into vertical panels, *c.* 1860.

1710-30

1730-50

1760-70

1770-90

1790-1830

1820

1830-50

1850-1900

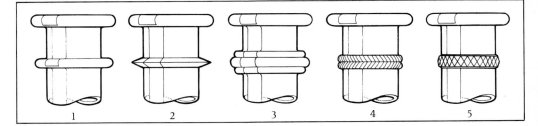

Above: **Decanter neck rings.**
1 Plain ring.
2 Triangular or knife-edge ring.
3 Triple or annulated ring.
4 Milled ring.
5 Cut or faceted ring.

Opposite: **The development of decanters**

had stoppers of glass. These were usually uncut ball or spire stoppers which were not always ground to fit the neck. The custom arose of having the name of the intended contents engraved in a cartouche upon the body, and these names include white wine, Madeira, Mountain (a Spanish wine from near Malaga) Port, Lisbon, Ale, and so on.

This tapering 'mallet' shape gave way to a similar style in which the body was wider at the shoulder than at the base, and cutting makes its appearance for the first time. This is usually in the form of diamond facet cutting on the body and neck, or neck only. The stoppers were cut to match.

From about 1800 onwards decanters evolved into the styles which are well known to collectors today. These are variations on a bulbous shape which has tapering shoulders leading to a short neck with a flange at the mouth, and anything from two to four equally spaced applied neck rings. They vary considerably in quality from the Irish ones which were thinly blown into shallow moulds, producing a flute moulded base to the richly ornate and heavily cut versions produced both in Ireland and England in the 1830's. During this period the two most popular stopper shapes were the flat round target or bulls eye and the mushroom. The former generally being used with the plainer decanters.

During the early years of the 1800's many coloured decanters were made which were usually sold in sets of three and were often gilded with imitation wine labels. The names used are generally those of spirits, usually Brandy, Rum and Hollands (gin). Whisky does not occur, since it was not generally drunk in England until the 1880's. These nineteenth century decanters are usually of two sizes. The small ones are not so popular today because it is claimed they do not take a whole bottle at one filling. This is because at the time they were popular, bottle sizes were based on the imperial pint and imperial quart. Our modern 26-ounce bottles fall between these two sizes.

As fashion has a habit of repeating itself, during the second half of the nineteenth century the globe and shaft decanter

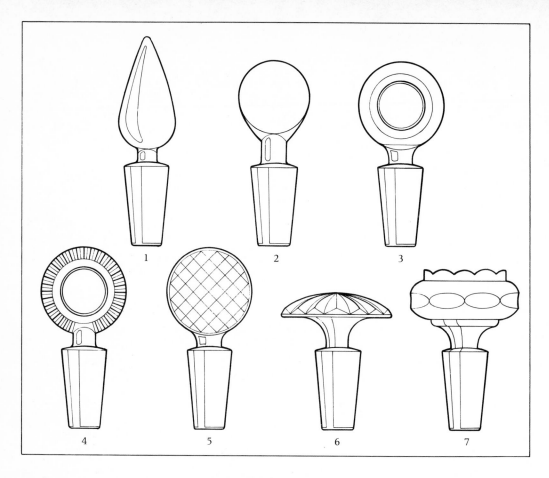

made its reappearance and, in a wide range of qualities, became the most popular decanter style of Victorian times.

The late Georgian era presents several other opportunities for exploring and collecting the wide variety present in a single type of vessel. Condiments and jelly glasses are two of them. Both of these were, of course, also made during the eighteenth century but there was a greater variety of them produced during the first half of the nineteenth century than either earlier or subsequently.

Condiments

The practice of seasoning food with made sauces and seasonings is a very old one. Not only did one add flavour to the food, but from the strength of some of them they undoubtedly also served the purpose of masking the flavour of food which may not have been very fresh. We know what some of these sauces were from the names engraved on silver labels or engraved or gilded on glass bottles. Kyan or cayenne, anchovy, lemon pickle and ketchup or catsup are just a few examples. The use

Decanter stoppers.
1 Spire stopper, plain or facet cut, 1760-80.
2 Lozenge stopper, 1760-1820.
3 Target or bull's eye stopper, 1780-1820.
4 Target stopper with radial grooves, cut or moulded, 1780-1820.
5 Flat round stopper with moulded cross-hatching, 1780-1820. This is often found on Irish decanters.
6 Mushroom stopper, cut or moulded, 1790-1840.
7 Hollow faceted stopper with a raised platform cut with radial grooves, 1830-50.

83 *Top left:* An unusual condiment set of five thinly blown wrythen bottles in a wooden stand, *c.* 1790.

84 *Top right:* Three salt cellars, all on 'lemon squeezer' feet, *c.* 1820.

85 *Above:* Three condiment bottles: (Left to right) Dry mustard bottle, *c.* 1800; Pepper bottle, *c.* 1830; Pepper bottle, *c.* 1820.

of these seasonings was not limited to any particular social class. Condiment sets were made to suit all pockets from the elegant cut glass sets on silver stands of the 1780's to the humble bottles that could be bought individually and knew no container. While complete sets are rare today and command good prices, individual bottles exhibiting all the well-known forms of cutting can be found at quite reasonable prices. Those cut with vertical panels, diamond facet cut bottles, bullseye cutting and various types of diamond cutting are only some of those which have survived.

At a more plebeian level there are many bottles on moulded pedestal feet which can be found individually to make up sets. These generally have bulbous bodies decorated with moulded vertical ribs. It was commonplace to cut small notches in these ribs, either on each or alternate ones. To match the bottles, which usually have pouring spouts, there are mustard pots which are shorter than the bottles. These have short wide necks with a flanged rim, and without their lids (which is usual) look like small Grecian urns. Mustard was generally used as dry, crushed seed, rather as we use black pepper today, and these pots are usually referred to as dry mustards. To match these there were salt cellars, usually with round oval bodies, with the same ribbed patterning as the bottles. Since oil and vinegar were also commonly used it would not be too difficult to assemble a reasonably matching set in this pattern, consisting of salt, mustard and several bottles.

I have mentioned the canoe-shaped salt cellars in connection with the diamond-shaped moulded pedestal feet, but there is one other type of salt cellar which is still fairly common: the monteith or bonnet glass. This consists of a small double ogee bowl of thick glass on a round foot. Some are decorated with cutting to the body and rim, but most have moulded patterns of diamonds or vertical ribs. The feet of these are sometimes roughly lobed to produce what is known as a petal foot.

When electroplating and mould-blown bottles became commonplace later in the nineteenth century, no home, however modest, need be without its cruet stand. However, the commercial sauce bottle seems to have put paid to the use of condiment bottles in recent years.

Jelly glasses

In these little glasses we have another example of domestic glassware which was widely used in the British Isles for two hundred years, but has now gone out of fashion. They fall into two distinct types: tall narrow bell-shaped bowls without stems but with plain or folded feet, and shallow cup-shaped bowls, invariably fitted with handles. Catalogues of the late nineteenth century differentiate between these two styles, calling the tall ones jelly glasses, while the cup-shaped ones are custard glasses.

During the eighteenth century the deep narrow bowl, decorated with various moulded patterns, was universally used, and these were sometimes fitted with one or two plain loop handles, and much more rarely, with double loop or B-handles. Although these glasses are generally referred to as

86 *Above:* An early jelly glass with double loop, or B, handles. There is a ball knop and a domed foot, c. 1740.

87 *Opposite top:* Three jelly glasses. (Left) Funnel bowl with a band of husk engraving, c. 1820. (Centre) A heavily cut bell bowl with an everted rim on a star cut foot, c. 1830. (Right) A bell bowl with a gadrooned base on a rudimentary stem and a plain foot, c. 1860. There was a brief revival in Venetian gadrooned decoration in this period.

88 *Opposite centre:* Two custard glasses, both c. 1850. (Left) A waisted bowl and ribbed base. (Right) A waisted gadrooned bowl.

89 *Opposite bottom:* Three custard glasses. The first has a bucket bowl and dates from 1840. The others both have cut bowls and date from 1870.

jelly or custard glasses I can find no reference to them under these names in contemporary lists. However, syllabub, or sillibub, glasses are mentioned quite commonly. A few of these glasses have spreading tops similar to the double ogee type of bowl, and I have had these represented to me as syllabub glasses, but my own opinion is that all these glasses were used as dessert glasses for any of these sweets. Syllabub is made of whipped cream flavoured with white wine and lemon. A whole range of creams or custards were made using egg yolks, milk or cream and flavourings. Jelly was made using calves feet, isinglass or hartshorn (obtained from the antlers of deer) and flavoured sweet or savoury according to its use. Sets of glasses containing these sweets were presented at table on glass stands or tazzas.

By the early nineteenth century the cup-shaped bowl, with no stem or foot, had become popular and these can usually be identified by the elaborate cutting, in the style of the period, which decorates them. During much of the century plain, tapering bowled custards with flared rim were in vogue and towards the end of the century the cup-shaped bowl on a short stem and plain foot makes its appearance. During the latter half of the nineteenth century there was a change in the way handles were applied to glass vessels. This is discussed on pp.

90 *Above:* An eighteenth century tazza, or comporte, showing how the custard and jelly glasses were served to the table. Victoria and Albert Museum, London.

91 *Opposite above:* Four 19th century green wine glasses showing typical styles covering the period 1810-80. Note how the shade of green varied considerably. Miss A. Cawardine.

92 *Opposite below:* An elaborately gilded set of decanters for Madeira, Burgundy and Champaigne with cut spire stoppers gilded to match. These names are unusual to find on the mock inscribed wine-labels applied to decanters from 1760 to 1830.

93 *Above:* A selection of opaque white glass enamelled with floral and chinoiserie subjects, all 1760-70. This type of glass was made in both Stourbridge and Bristol, and the floral decoration is often associated with Michael Edkins, who worked in both places (pages 107 and 113). This type of ware was made in imitation of porcelain and the small vases are some of the earliest examples of glassware made for decorative rather than utilitarian purposes.

94 *Left:* A dark-blue cut butter dish with a domed lid, *c.* 1800. The style of cutting suggests this could have been made in Ireland, and to many people the colour would suggest a Bristol origin. My comments in the text on these areas of glassmaking will show the difficulty of making a definite attribution. Miss A. Cawardine.

95 An early eighteenth century tazza with a baluster stem consisting of an annulated knop over an inverted baluster and a domed and folded foot, c. 1725.

144 and 152 but it is interesting to note that alone of all the glass of the late Victorian period the fashion persisted of applying the handles to custard glasses in the older manner.

Toddy lifters and stirrup cups

Two small novelty items are associated with this period. They are the toddy lifter and the stirrup cup. Toddy lifters, which usually look like small, long-necked decanters with a hole in the middle of the base, work on the same principle as a pipette. The thick end is immersed in the punch or toddy, it fills under atmospheric pressure, the thumb is placed over the hole in the neck, which prevents the liquid immediately running out again, and then it can be transferred to the glass. When the thumb is removed from the neck the liquid then falls into the intended receptacle. These curiosities were made in a variety of patterns and according to Percy Bate in his book on glass published in 1913, they were peculiarly Scottish. I had never seen any corroborative evidence for this until reading *Notes on a Cellar Book* by G. Saintbury. In a footnote on page 116, relating to toddy made in Scotland, he says 'you do not swig it brutally from the rummer or tumbler, but ladle it genteelly, as required, with a special instrument made and provided for the purpose, into a wine glass . . .' That sounds to me remarkably like a toddy lifter.

Stirrup glasses or cups are usually funnel-bowled wine glasses with a stem but no foot. This leads to suspicions that

they are glasses which have had the feet broken off. There is a good general test to discover whether this is likely. Stand the glass on the end of its stem and try to imagine it with a foot. Would it then conform to the general size and proportion of conventional wine glasses of the period? With true stirrup glasses the answer to this is always 'No', since the bowl is always large in relation to the stem. In other words, it would look top heavy as an ordinary drinking glass. In addition, the stem often terminates in a large facet cut knop which again would be out of character if it were followed immediately by a plain foot. Stirrup glasses were used from the 1830's onwards and are difficult things to date, since they vary little over the years. Their use at hunt meets accounts for their 'gimmicky' nature, since riders on horseback presumably had nowhere they could stand a wine glass with a foot. They are also sometimes called coaching glasses, suggesting that passengers on the outside of the coach could have something warming before starting their journey.

96 *Left:* Two funnel-bowled stirrup cups, *c.* 1840.

97 *Above:* Three toddy lifters, *c.* 1830. The first one has been made to resemble a wine glass but notice the hole running through the stem.

98 *Opposite above left:* A glass tankard with its body divided by two horizontal applied collars. This style of decoration was used widely in Germany in the seventeenth century on a type of glass called a 'Pasglas'.

99 *Opposite above right:* A tankard with a gadrooned base and a strap handle, *c.* 1850.

Coloured glass

'Coloured glass' tends to mean slightly different things to different people. To the collector whose interest is centred on drinking glasses of the eighteenth and early nineteenth centuries it is strictly as a term for coloured utilitarian wares. The collector whose interest lies in the late nineteenth century sees it as relating to colour used purely as a decorative

100 *Above:* An oil lamp,
c. 1860. The globular
reservoir held the oil with
the wick showing through a
metal plate on top. The
handle has a thumb grip; the
stem is fixed to a base which
has an upturned rim,
presumably to catch any
drips.

expression of the wealth of ornamental glass produced during
that period. It could be said that the subject is particularly
relevant to the years covered in this chapter, since it was
during the early 1800's that colour became a dominant feature
in glassware. Let us consider, then, the history of the use of
colour in British glass and treat it as a bridge from the
utilitarian to the purely decorative.

The knowledge of, and the ability to produce, colours in
glass is as old as the art of glassmaking itself. In ancient Egypt,
yellow, blue, green and purple, as well as white, were all
colours employed to decorate the small bottles and jars which
have been found by modern excavators. The Portland Vase,
dating from the first century A.D. is an example of blue glass
covered or cased with a layer of white glass. The Venetian
glassmakers of the sixteenth and seventeenth centuries produced glass of every hue, including multi-coloured glass in
perfect imitation of agate and chalcedony. Neri's *L'Arte
Vitrearia* of 1612 gives the recipes for producing every possible
shade of colour in glass. The other important use for coloured
glass had been for windows, principally in churches. This was
an art which had continued in Britain since earliest times.

Although this knowledge was readily available, it was left to
European glassmakers to exploit the use of colour in domestic
glass, and even during the eighteenth century when British
glassmaking reigned supreme, it was largely disregarded in this
country. Could it be that the English Glass Sellers and their

customers were so obsessed with the clarity and brilliance of their lead crystal that there was no demand for coloured glass?

Some coloured glass was made, however. One or two globe and shaft decanters made of lead glass and coloured a rich amethyst are attributed to the Ravenscroft period, and one or two early eighteenth century green wine glasses are typical of the baluster and Silesian stem period. However, coloured glasses datable before 1750 are rare. From that date all the principal styles are represented by coloured examples: plain stems, opaque and air twist stems and facet stems, but they remain rare. There are variations among the opaque twist stems, some having clear stems with a white twist, but coloured bowls and feet that are either blue or green. It is interesting to note that while blue, green and purple glasses were made, no yellow or red ones from before 1845 have been identified. The use of threads of colour in opaque twist glasses has already been discussed (see page 59).

From about 1800, and for the next forty years, coloured drinking glasses and decanters were very popular, and most of the coloured glassware to be found today was made during that period. The two most popular styles for coloured drinking glasses were the funnel bowl on a short stem having a central blade knop, and the tulip shape bowl on a plain stem. These survived until about 1830 when styles changed, and in the same way that light baluster glasses had developed from the heavy balusters a century earlier, the coloured wine glasses became lighter, taller and the stems had either ball knops or baluster shapes. These were followed by slender plain stems. In addition to the blue, green and amethyst glasses of this period, brown was also used. It produced glasses ranging from pale amber to a rich caramel brown.

Coloured decanters have already been referred to but a curiosity is that while green wine glasses are common and blue ones are rare, the reverse is true of decanters with the blue ones considerably outnumbering the green ones.

The other colour which was produced during the eighteenth century was opaque white. We have noted its use as the white twisted decoration in the stems of wine glasses, but it was also used in the 1760's to produce glass in imitation of porcelain. At that time porcelain was beginning to be made in England, but it was expensive. By colouring their glass with arsenic or tin oxide the glassmakers could produce a dense opaque white glass which bore a striking resemblance to porcelain. The similarity was enhanced by employing porcelain decorators to paint it. Among these opaque white pieces are some of the earliest glass articles which were more decorative than useful: hanging wall baskets shaped like cornucopiae and small baluster vases to stand on sideboards or mantels.

I have no doubt that many of my readers will be wondering why I have discussed coloured glass at such length without mentioning the name of Bristol. Glass is generally such anonymous stuff and its place of origin unknown that collectors love to have a name to use as a peg on which to hang their acquisitions, and Bristol is the name which is constantly pressed into use as the origin of all coloured glass. I have seen glass of every colour and period represented as Bristol glass, but the facts don't really bear out these sweeping attributions. Coloured glass was undoubtedly made in Bristol, but the Bristol glassmakers had no monopoly. Coloured glass was also made in London, the Midlands and Newcastle, and references to coloured glass made in these areas pre-date the first reference to blue glass made in Bristol, which occurs in the ledgers of Michael Edkins, a decorator of ceramics and glass. In 1763 he recorded 'To gilding four blue jars and beakers for 2/-'. He also recorded work carried out for Lazarus Jacobs, who by 1793 was listed in the Bristol Directory as a 'glass merchant in Avon St.'.

In 1805 Isaac Jacobs (son of Lazarus) opened the Non-Such Flint Glass Manufactory and advertised that he manufactured 'every article in the glass line'. In the following year he again advertised glass, adding 'Coats of Arms, Crests and Cyphers done upon the same in the greatest style, by some of the first artists in the Kingdom . . .' Jacobs is important since a number

101 A perfume bottle, c. 1770. It has fired gilt decoration on faceted blue glass and was made in Bristol. Pilkington Glass Museum, St Helens.

of pieces of coloured glass survive, decorated with gilding and marked underneath I. Jacobs, Bristol. These are usually plates or finger bowls bearing a gilded Greek key pattern. It is generally thought that Jacobs was the decorator, but from the above advertisements it is clear that he employed decorators and had his name marked on the product in the same way that Absolom was doing in Yarmouth at the same period.

The only other coloured glass which can be definitely attributed to Bristol are several items marked Wadham Ricketts & Co., who were owners of the Phoenix Glass Works from 1785.

These definite attributions have been largely responsible for linking the name of Bristol so strongly with coloured glass, but there is one other reason which I think has had even more influence, for I am certain that this association is not a recent one, developed in recent years with the enormous increase in interest in old glass. Many people talk of the distinctive purplish tinge in blue glass which proves a Bristol origin. This colour was achieved by using, as a colouring agent, cobalt oxide imported from Saxony. Cobalt had been mixed there from the sixteenth century when it was found that a treated oxide of cobalt called smalt was ideal for producing a blue dye for decorating pottery and for producing a rich blue tint in glass. During the eighteenth century this was imported into England through the port of Bristol, and differing authorities say that it was sold by auction there, or that the supply was controlled by William Cookson, a wholesale druggist in Bristol. There were periods when supplies were interrupted and the glassmakers had to turn to alternative supplies which did not produce such satisfactory results. The quality of the Saxon smalt, then, was such that it was in demand wherever glass was made, and since the sole source of supply in Britain was through Bristol it is quite reasonable to assume that 'Bristol blue' became a widespread hallmark of quality in coloured glass. Link this with marked pieces known to have originated in Bristol and a myth is born.

Glassmaking in Bristol was at its height during the eighteenth century when up to fifteen glasshouses were working, but by 1833 this had declined to four, and by 1900 they had virtually disappeared. If Bristol can claim any special distinction in coloured glassmaking it is for the dense white opaque glass for which it acquired a reputation, rather than the blue and green glass which was made everywhere. The Bristol flint glasshouses also produced the full range of clear and cut glass in all the styles of the eighteenth century and also had a

102 *Above:* A striped jug of the Nailsea type, *c.* 1800. The glass made at the Nailsea factory became so popular that it was widely imitated, making a definite identification of the place of manufacture almost impossible. Victoria and Albert Museum, London.

103 *Above right:* Nailsea bottle of green bottle glass with white trailed threads and an applied loop handle, *c.* 1830.

flourishing bottle glass industry which exported vast quantities of bottles to the West Indies and North America.

The mention of bottles brings us onto the other famous glasshouse of the Bristol area which has captured a place in the popular mythology of glass collectors, the Nailsea Glass Company. This was started at Nailsea, a village some miles south-west of Bristol, in 1788 by John Robert Lucas, who came of a Bristol glassmaking family. It was essentially a bottle glasshouse which established a high reputation in that art. It is better known, however, for a variety of domestic articles made of bottle glass but enlivened with flecks or threads of coloured glass. Among these are rolling pins, carafes and jugs. One or two sealed bottles are also known, one of which is dated 1837. These wares are also attributed to a glasshouse at Wrockwardine in Shropshire.

By extension, all decorative glass objects with threads or flecks of colour have become associated with the name, so that now any flask, pipe, rolling pin, hat or other purely ornamental piece of coloured glass is labelled Nailsea. The glasshouse was controlled for many years by the Chance family who were famous glassmakers in the Bristol area and later in Birmingham. A descendant of that family, Sir Hugh Chance, has effectively proved the fallacy of this idea, and it is now accepted that such articles were more generally made in the north of England. The Nailsea glasshouse continued in production until 1869 when it finally closed down.

Chapter 5

Methods of decorating glassware

Many different methods of decorating glass have been practised over the centuries. Several of them, such as gilding and enamelling, are also carried out on other materials, but glass, because of its transparency, lends itself uniquely to two methods, those of cutting and engraving.

It is perhaps an indication of the sophistication which glassmaking achieved in the past that almost every important technique for decorating glass was already known 2000 years ago. Many of these died out with the decline of the Roman Empire, and were only rediscovered during the eighteenth and nineteenth centuries.

There are basically two methods of decorating glass—that which is incorporated during its manufacture and is therefore an integral part of the glass, and that which is applied subsequently.

The former was in the control of the glassmaker and included the use of such devices as the knops of baluster stems and the twisted patterns in opaque and air twist stems. Drawing on the inventiveness of the Venetian glassmakers of the sixteenth and seventeenth centuries the English glassmakers also applied threads of glass to their products to embellish them. These were either simply wound round the body of the glass, or were drawn into patterns resembling chains or diamonds. This latter was the 'nipt diamond waies' pattern of Ravenscroft's price list. Thicker threads of glass were added, and then shaped with patterned pincers. The bowls of glasses were blown into moulds to produce particular patterns such as hexagons or ribs, or to receive indented moulding around the base: flutes, dimples, diamonds, etc. All these were to improve the aesthetic appeal of the article, and can therefore be termed decorative techniques.

All other methods of decorating were added by craftsmen working outside the glasshouse, and usually in the employ of the glass sellers. Let us consider these techniques and see how they differ from the same methods used in Europe.

Gilding

This was a decorating method which never achieved the same degree of popularity in Britain that it did in Europe. In fact, what popularity it commanded seems to have been prompted by gilded glassware imported from Germany in about 1750. Robert Dossie in his *Handmaid to the Arts* published in 1758 describes at length methods of gilding employed both in Britain and Germany. There were two principal methods: oil gilding and fired gilding. In the former gold powder or leaf was applied over an oil or varnish-based size, which was then burnished. This was applied either to plain surfaces or to heighten engraved decoration. In either case the fixing medium tended to be water soluble, so the gilding was easily removed during normal use. Where it was applied over engraving usually the only evidence of it now is a discoloration caused by the fixing medium rather than the gold.

Fired gilding, on the other hand, was always applied to plain surfaces and heated in the annealing furnaces to produce, when burnished, a firm, durable film of gold. This lasted very well and the small amount of gilding which survives today was executed in this method. Dossie complained that many glasses were gilded in Britain by the oil process in imitation of the German ones, but the poor durability of the gold gave this method of decoration a bad name.

Only one or two names have come down to us as exponents of the art of gilding. James Giles, who had a workshop in London, and is probably better known as a decorator on porcelain, is credited with many fine examples of gilding on scent bottles, decanters and vases. His use of gilded insects has a parallel on early porcelain plates, where they were used to cover blemishes in the firing or glazing. Sprays of flowers and chinoiserie decoration are also motifs attributed to Giles.

I have already referred to Isaac Jacobs in the section on coloured glass, and although it is his name which appears on several gilded pieces it is unlikely that he carried out the work personally. It is more probable that he had a decorating workshop employing both enamellers and gilders.

Michael Edkins, who is better known as an enameller, also carried out gilding, as shown by the ledger entry (page 107).

William Absolom of Great Yarmouth was a retailer of pottery, porcelain and glass from the 1780's to about 1815. A number of glasses have survived, mostly square based rummers and barrel shaped tumblers which carry gilt inscriptions and pictures relating to Great Yarmouth. These frequently have views of Yarmouth Church or a particular type of two-wheeled carriage known as a Yarmouth cart. Other subjects refer to specific persons, associations or regiments. Very rarely these are marked underneath 'Absolom, Yarm 25' referring to his address at No. 25 Market Row. Many of these gilded subjects also appear as engravings on other glasses, but these will be dealt with later.

This flat gilding, practised in Britain, takes its influence from the German style. Gilding in France was of a somewhat different nature since it was more thickly applied and during the nineteenth century when French glassmaking started to achieve some distinction it developed almost to an encrusted technique, with the gilding standing proud of the surface.

Enamelling

Painting in coloured enamels on glass had been practised in Venice and Germany from the late sixteenth century onwards, and in Germany had been brought to a very high standard. As with gilding, it was not until the middle of the eighteenth century, however, that it seems to have made any impact as a decorative technique in Britain. Thorpe suggests that applied decorative techniques in this country were in response to the Excise Act of 1745 which inhibited the glassmakers from expressing themselves in glass. My own feeling is that the demand was as much the result of changing taste which expressed itself in all domestic articles during the reign of George III.

Enamelling, like gilding, was applied by two different methods. Cold enamelling was simply painted on glass. This was a quick and cheap method, but suffered from the fact that it was easily rubbed off. It was used mostly on cheaper goods and it is unusual, these days, to find examples which have survived in good condition. This technique was used on jug and basin sets which were popular in the early 1800's. The decoration was generally floral or consisted of mottoes like 'Be canny with the cream' or 'Remember the Giver'. Much cold enamelling was also applied to the decorative rolling pins which the sailors on the coastal ships reputedly bought in the north of England and decorated during their voyages to sell at their ports of call. The decoration on these was often a combination of freehand enamelling and applied transfers which were over-painted.

The other, more important, method of enamelling, dates back to the mid-eighteenth century when several decorators used a vitreous enamel which became permanent when the

112

104 A typical Jacobite pair of wine glasses of the mid-eighteenth century, bearing the portrait of Charles Edward Stuart. Victoria and Albert Museum, London.

glass was reheated. The two artists whose names are known to us, Michael Edkins and William Beilby, both worked at some time in the Birmingham area where Bilston was renowned for its enamelling trade. They both learned the art there; Edkins then going to Bristol in about 1762 and Beilby setting up his enamelling workshop in Newcastle-on-Tyne in 1760. As they were both of a similar age I wonder if they knew each other before going their separate ways?

Quite a lot is known about Edkins. Some of his ledgers and notebooks have survived and family history was passed on to succeeding generations. At various times he worked as a decorator of Bristol pottery and as a coach and carriage painter before turning his hand to decorating on glass. He painted and gilded for several of the Bristol glass manufacturers including Lazarus Jacobs (father of Isaac) in the mid-1780's. It is difficult to connect his name with any particular item, but by association with articles of pottery he is known to have decorated several pieces of glass painted with sprays of flowers, and birds have also been attributed to him. The finest painting of this period occurs on the opaque white tea caddies and vases for

113

which Bristol is well known. Another favourite subject was chinoiserie decoration showing figures in Chinese dress; the colours are always brilliant and reminiscent of porcelain decoration of the period.

By contrast, William Beilby seems to have confined himself to decorating on glass right from the beginning of his independent career. It is interesting that as late as 1925 the major books dealing with glass made no reference to Beilby and generally attributes his glasses to a Bristol origin. Since then, however, several glasses signed by him have come to light and modern research has given him due credit for his work.

Beilby's work falls into two main categories: commercial work which consists mainly of standard wine glasses of the period decorated in white enamel with a variety of motifs which were repeated many times, and his commissioned work. Among the former are pieces with the grape and vine leaf border, the classical ruins and architectural studies, the sporting and rural pursuits series. Very rarely the rural scenes are executed in a limited colour palette of green, yellow and aubergine. The grape and vine leaf glasses are repetitious, although occasionally the grapes are executed in a pale purple colour. The pictorial glasses are always charming, with the rural scenes showing some affinity with the later wood-engraved vignettes of country life executed by Thomas Bewick, who was apprenticed to William's brother Ralph Beilby. These scenes show huntsmen, anglers, rowers and shepherds.

Beilby's sister Mary is also known to have executed some of the decoration on these little glasses, and much effort has been devoted to trying to distinguish which hand was at work on particular glasses. It is probable, however, that there were other people at work enamelling on glass in Newcastle at this period. Thomas Bewick wrote a memoir of his life which was published in 1862, some years after his death, after careful editing by his daughters. On page 56 of this book there is the following reference:

'. . . and the latter (William) taught his brother Thomas and sister Mary enamelling and painting and, in this way, this most respectable and industrious family lived together and maintained themselves'.

Later:

'He (brother Ralph, an engraver) had also assisted his brother and sister in their constant employment of enamel painting on glass'.

More interesting is the text as Bewick originally wrote it,

which was not published until 1975. In this is a reference which does not appear in the 'official' memoir of 1862:
'In my attendance at the work shop of Gilbert (Gilbert Gray, a book binder) I got acquainted with several young men who like myself, admired him – but one of the most singular of these was Anthony Taylor, a glass maker – he was a keen admirer of drawings and paintings but had no opportunity of shewing his talents in the Arts, otherwise than in his paintings and his enamellings on glass, in which way, considering his situation he was proficient'.

Although most of the 'Beilby' glasses are in a closely similar style, and cover the range of subjects I have mentioned, there occasionally appears an enamelled glass in an obviously different hand, and sometimes with enamel of a different quality. With these three names given by Bewick, the question of attribution becomes more difficult.

The commission work that Beilby carried out was usually more elaborate than his commercial work, and often applied in coloured enamels. Among these are glasses inscribed with references to particular groups or individuals, such as 'Success to the Swordmakers' dated 1767, and 'Thos Brown, Nenthead, 1769'. Many of the commissions were for armourial decoration on large goblets which required the use of a wide variety of colours. The Beilby colours are much more subtle than those found in the Bristol enamelling, with a delicate gradation of shade to give the decoration some modelling. The best known of these are the bucket bowled opaque twist goblets with the Royal coat of arms, the Prince of Wales feathers and Beilby's signature, thought to have been produced in 1762 to commemorate the birth of the future George IV.

The Beilbys pursued their profession until about 1770 when they seem to have left Newcastle.

One other small group of glasses is known which has enamelled decoration, and those have a portrait of Bonnie Prince Charlie in Highland dress, executed in coloured enamels. The draughtsmanship is crude when compared with any other enamelling on glass, and may be the work of an amateur.

Cutting

The decoration of glass by cutting is a process that produces highly polished, deeply indented geometric patterns. This process is unique to glass because the refractive property of light passing through it enhances what might otherwise seem a dull, mechanical form of decoration. Glass has been cut from earliest times, and during the seventeenth and eighteenth centuries German decorators developed it to a very high standard, using as their medium the hard, white soda/lime glass which the glassmakers of that country had developed.

When Ravenscroft's lead glass became popular and generally made in Britain it was not long before its advantages as a material for cutting became apparent. Its softness made it easy to cut, and its clarity meant that thicker sections, to carry deep cutting, could be produced. Also, the addition of lead altered the refractive property of the glass so that the cut surfaces produced brilliant prismatic effects. There was little or no experience of cutting in this country because the Venetian tradition on which our industry had grown up depended on a thinly blown product unsuitable for the cutter's wheel. The earliest cutters were German craftsmen imported to work for the glass sellers here. Several early baluster stem glasses have survived decorated with cutting in the German manner; the bowls cut with vertical panels and the knops covered with diamond facets.

The *London Gazette* of 18 October 1709 carried an advertisement which stated, 'There is lately brought over a great parcel of very fine German cut and carved glasses . . .'. Thereafter advertisements for cut glass appear regularly indicating that there was always a market for it. With the imposition of the Excise Duty in 1745 cut glass became an expensive luxury and most of the articles from that period onwards are in the luxury class: chandeliers, girandoles, sweetmeat glasses and salvers.

After the granting of free trade to Ireland in 1780 it is noticeable that the Irish glasshouses which sprang up in response to the opportunity did not have to 'invent' cut glass but imported their equipment and labour from England, which shows that it was a continuing, if exclusive, tradition.

The cutting process consists of marking out a piece of plain blown glass, known as a 'blank' and then roughing out the pattern on a coarse wheel of sandstone or iron on to which was directed a stream of sand and water. This rough pattern was finished to the desired limits and rough polished with a finer wheel, and the resulting design polished with a buffing wheel coated with putty powder or jeweller's rouge. In the early twentieth century a method of polishing called acid polishing was developed whereby the entire surface of the vessel was lightly etched by an acid which produced a bright surface finish. Since this acid attacked the whole surface evenly it is possible to distinguish between this treatment and the earlier hand polishing. Polishing by hand produces sharp crisp edges and it is usually possible to see the 'flow line' produced by the uniform direction of the polishing wheel. Acid polishing removes the sharp edges of the design and leaves a uniform finish over the whole surface.

In the later 1800's it was quite normal for cut glass to be press-moulded to bypass the roughing process so that only a light cut and the polishing processes were required, thus saving time and money.

Various cutting patterns were discussed in the chapter on Irish glass, and the diagram on page 83 illustrates the principal ones used in both countries.

Engraving

Engraving, although it is a form of cutting carried out on a wheel, is a quite different technique from cutting. Engraving is the abrasion of the surface of the glass to produce a roughened area which forms an inscription or a pictorial design. In other words, engraving is a form of writing or drawing on glass which can be carried out in one of two ways – either on a small copper wheel with a shaped profile which is fed with an abrasive compound, or freehand with a sharp pointed tool such as a diamond.

Engraving with a point also can be carried out by two methods, a straightforward line technique as if drawing with a pencil, and another technique known as stipple engraving in which the artist lightly taps the surface of the glass with a point

105 *Below:* A large bucket-bowl rummer engraved to commemorate the establishment of the Steam Engine Makers Society in November 1824. It bears engravings of a steam railway engine, a steam sailing ship and a beam engine.

106 *Below right:* A pressed tankard commemorating the iron bridge over the River Wear at Sunderland, *c.* 1825.

to produce a series of minute dots. The density of these dots gives effects of light and shade so that the areas with least dots seem darkest while a close pattern of dots produces the light areas. This is an extremely difficult method of engraving and has only ever had a very few good practitioners.

The earliest English glasses which carry engraving are all examples of diamond point work. Nearly all the surviving examples from the Verzelini glasshouse are decorated with inscriptions and designs using this technique. Wheel engraving, as with other methods of decoration, seems to have been imported here during the eighteenth century from Germany where it had been in common use for a hundred years or more. Engraving never reached a particularly high standard in the British Isles during the eighteenth century, although a distinct improvement can be seen in nineteenth century glasses such as the Sunderland Bridge rummers and various sporting goblets. It is interesting that the best engraving on glass ever produced in this country is being done today by a number of very fine artist engravers. During the eighteenth century the only engraving which could compare with this modern art was carried out by Dutch engravers who achieved most of their best work on English glass. The wheel-engraved work of Jacob Sang is so detailed and delicate that it hardly seems possible that it could have been done freehand by human agency. The stipple engraving of Wolff and Greenwood is so delicate as to be invisible from some angles but brilliant and full of subtle gradation when looked at from the right point of view.

One of the important contributions of engraved decoration is that so much of it was commemorative. Apart from the aesthetic qualities of the engraving such a great deal refers to particular people, places and events. These often serve to define the period when the object was made and thereby give us a reference point to date similar vessels. Collecting commemorative glass is a most worthwhile hobby since one not only learns something of military, political and economic history but at the same time one has reliable evidence for dating the glass.

While many inscriptions refer to known persons or events many others were engraved for private individuals about whose lives we can learn little. But many are dated, and this is the important thing. The following is a list of some of the main subjects commemorated.

Royalty Every monarch from Charles II onwards is referred to on glass. A tall seventeenth century ale flute bears a portrait of Charles II and the inscription 'God Bless King Charles the

107 *Opposite above:* Three examples of George Davidson's *Pearline* glass. The white areas are achieved by partial reheating. *Pearline* glass was made from 1889 onwards. Miss A. Cawardine.

108 *Opposite below:* Four wine glasses having colour twist stems, all *c.* 1760. The green and blue pattern of the extreme left example is rare. These English glasses should not be confused with the Continental colour twist glasses which are much more common.

109 *Opposite above left:* Two examples of the revival of the Venetian style. Both were made by James Powell's Whitefriars Glassworks in the 1880's. (Left) A tall ale flute with a hollow quatrefoil knop. (Right) A small beaker decorated with applied threads of glass.

110 *Opposite above right:* An overlay vase by Thomas Webb & Sons in a pseudo-cameo technique *c.* 1926. The relief is achieved by acid etching (page 123). Miss A. Cawardine.

111 *Opposite below:* A pair of white vases transfer-printed with Greek classical scenes, a style much in vogue in the 1860's and 1870's. This pair is marked 'Geo. Bacchus and Son'. Miss A. Cawardine.

112 A pressed tankard commemorating the opening of the high level railway bridge over the Tyne in 1850.

Second'. George I is remembered on the four-sided Silesian stem glasses moulded with the words 'God Save the King G.R.'. Queen Victoria's Golden and Diamond Jubilees are remembered on innumerable pressed plates.

Historical events William III's victory in Ireland is found on glasses bearing the words 'To The Immortal Memory' and 'Battle of the Boyne 1 July 1690.'. Every one of Nelson's naval battles may be found mentioned on glass.

Personalities Nelson and Wellington are remembered on many glasses. Admiral Byng, who lost Minorca to the French and was executed in 1757, Admiral Keppel, the Duke of Leinster, Edmund Burke and William Pitt are among many famous people to be found illustrated on drinking glasses.

Political There are many electioneering glasses commemorating candidates for Parliament. Jacobite glasses cover several groups. Many recall the Jacobite cause, some carry portraits of Charles Edward Stuart (Bonnie Prince Charlie) while others were engraved for clubs or societies with Jacobite sympathies; the Society of Sea Serjeants and the Beefeaters Club.

'Wilkes and Liberty' on a glass remembers John Wilkes who attacked the Government in his newspaper *The North Briton* in the 1760's and who, in spite of being gaoled, was elected to Parliament. Other glasses rail against particular taxes and are inscribed 'No Excise'.

On pressed glass can be found references to Gladstone, Disraeli and the Congress of Vienna in 1882.

Industrial One glass has a whaling scene on it; others wish success to 'The Coal Trade', 'The Wool Trade', 'Agriculture' and so on. Several glasses refer to canals, and another which I possessed several years ago was engraved to mark the founding of the 'Steam Engine Makers Society' in 1824.

Bridges were a favourite subject. Everyone has heard of the Sunderland Bridge rummers. This bridge was the largest single-span, vast-iron bridge built in this country. It spanned the Wear at Sunderland and was opened in 1796. Other bridges commemorated are the Scarborough high level bridge and the Newcastle high level bridge which is featured on a press-moulded tankard. Several small glasses recall pit and colliery disasters in which varying numbers of miners lost their lives. These are always cheap glasses coarsely engraved. They were presumably owned by the families of the victims. I wonder how this tradition arose?

Sporting Several hunts and huntsmen are mentioned on glass. Boxers, racehorses and jockeys also feature. Henry Greener of Sunderland produced a pressed glass tankard to honour

Edward Hanlon, an oarsman who was World Champion sculler in 1880, when he beat Edward Trickett of Australia. This same tankard was re-issued two years later with a slightly altered inscription when he beat Boyd of England.

General Under this heading we may group all those glasses which bear names or initials of ordinary people. Some also have the name of a public house and one may imagine a regular customer insisting on using his own named glass. Sometimes a pair of glasses carries the names of a man and woman and the same date, surely to commemorate their wedding. One mid-eighteenth century glass which passed through my hands was roughly engraved in diamond point 'D. G. died 1826 aged 93 years'. Had D. G. owned that glass since it was new some seventy years earlier?

The practice of commemorating people and events is not dead. A number of modern glasses have been decorated to celebrate Churchill, the Royal Silver Wedding Anniversary, Prince Charles on being made Prince of Wales, the first American space capsule and various boroughs and cathedrals. While many of these may be of doubtful value as investments currently, two hundred years from now I am sure that those which survive will be highly prized. To handle a piece of glass decorated with a reference to some well-known person or event of the past, knowing that it was made and decorated when the subject was alive, or the event topical, gives me a stronger feeling of history and a closer relationship with the past than anything else I know. This must also be the fascination for many people, and account for the high prices which such pieces command when they appear in the sale rooms.

One of the reasons why so many people, places and events are remembered on engraved glass is that it was such an ideal medium for decoration. It was widely and readily available at all price levels, it was a durable material, it didn't require much equipment to carry out the decoration which could be applied anywhere at any time, and it required no subsequent finishing treatments. By contrast, decoration on pottery and porcelain required the availability of glazing equipment and kilns for firing. The potting process did not lend itself so well to the production of 'one-off' pieces. Commemorative scenes and inscriptions engraved on silver and gold were only for the wealthier classes, and in any case would not display as well as decorated glassware.

There is much confusion between wheel engraving and the acid process described next. Although the general appearance

113 *Top:* Electioneering glass. Its ogee bowl is inscribed 'Sir Francis Knollys and Liberty 1761'. In that year Knollys was returned to Parliament as MP for Reading.

114 *Above:* A privateer glass. The bucket bowl reads 'Success to the Defiance privateer'. The glass has an opaque-twist stem and a plain foot. The Defiance sailed from Bristol.

115 *Top:* A sporting goblet. The round funnel bowl is engraved with a fox hunting scene and the words 'Prosperity to Fox Hunting'. The unusual air twist stem has knops at shoulder and base, *c.* 1760.

116 *Above:* An opaque-twist wine glass engraved in the manner of David Wolff. Two mannikins clasp hands and drink a toast.

is often similar, there are distinct differences. Close inspection with a magnifying glass will show the individual strokes of the engraver's wheel quite clearly. Acid etching produces an even finish on the decorated area free from the variations of depth associated with wheel engraving. The outline of acid etched areas is also much more sharply defined than on engraved glasses.

Acid etching

This is another process which originated in Europe and was only taken up generally in this country very much later. The earliest known piece of glass decorated with acid was made in Germany, and dated 1686. It is not known exactly what sort of acid was used, but with the discovery of hydrofluoric acid in Sweden around 1770 a most effective medium for etching glass came into being.

The method generally used was to cover the vessel in an acid resistant varnish, the desired decoration was inscribed through this coating to expose the glass, which was then subjected to attack by acid. After the correct depth of pattern was achieved the acid was washed off and the varnish dissolved. An English example dated 1783 survives using this technique. This method proved nearly as laborious as engraving, but eventually two faster methods were developed for producing the decoration. One was in effect a transfer on paper which could be produced in quantity from an engraved plate. Instead of printing ink the transfer was coated with the masking varnish which could be applied in one go to the glass. This was then dipped 'in acid, and after the removal of the varnish the subject of the transfer appeared on the glass. This method had some currency from about 1840 to 1860. In about 1860 John Northwood of Stourbridge introduced a semi-mechanical process for acid etching. This was a form of copying machine in which a pointer traced round a master pattern transferred the design to a needle in contact with a varnish-covered glass. This meant that quite elaborate patterns could be copied exactly many times with little skill required from the operator. Patterns produced in this way are distinctive because the outline, when viewed through a magnifying glass, is of an even width and depth.

Northwood subsequently developed a machine for producing geometric patterns directly onto the vessels covered with protective varnish, and these were produced in large quantities well into this century. The Greek key pattern was one of the most popular achieved by this method.

Chapter 6

Victorian glassmaking

In 1833 a Commission on Glass Industries had investigated the state of the trade. Although it had reported its parlous condition, it took until 1845 before declining revenues from the punitive Excise Duty made the Government feel that the return did not justify the cost of collection and withdraw it. While the Excise Duty was in force no glassmaker could call his business his own. Every step in the process was under the control and supervision of the Exciseman resident in the glassworks. The withdrawal of the Excise Duty, followed by the Great Exhibition of 1851, signalled both an ending and a beginning.

What ended was the orderly progression from one style of glassmaking or decorative fashion to another, which had endured for a hundred and fifty years, during which time the glass sellers had largely dictated the direction in which domestic glassware had developed, and the manufacturers had claimed that the Excise Duty had inhibited experimentation.

The new beginning was initially a reaction which set in when the relief from Excise Duty encouraged the glassmakers into a new exuberance because the amount of metal in any article they made was no longer limited by financial considerations. This led to deeper and more elaborate cutting which found its culmination in the Exhibition of 1851. Some of the glassware shown there was technically marvellous but totally impractical. At the same time English glassmakers began experimenting with the decorative techniques then popular in Europe; the use of coloured glass, coloured overlays, opaline glass and so on. The Great Exhibition brought many manufacturers of these wares to England, and the public was introduced to a diversity of decorative glassware that it had not seen before. Some of these caught the public imagination, and the English glassmakers, realising the potential business to be done, and looking for outlets for their new-found freedom of expression, seized upon these foreign styles and started to diversify as they had never done before. When new techniques were required such as the overlaying of one colour upon another, or the very individual styles of decoration which made these foreign wares attractive, they did not hesitate to import foreign craftsmen from whom they could learn these new skills.

The results of all this were an infusion of new blood into the industry, a widening of the variety of glass being made, a new approach to glassmaking which placed the emphasis on decorative effect for its own sake and, most far-reaching, a strong tendency of the glass companies to be the originators of ideas and new styles, so that production, decoration and distribution were all controlled by one source. Arising from these circumstances the British glass industry of the second half of the nineteenth century became a major manufacturing industry which exercised an important influence on domestic style and taste. It is this movement and these companies that we shall look at during this chapter.

The Great Exhibition of 1851 was held in a building specially built for the purpose. The glassmakers played an important part in its construction and decoration, as well as featuring among the exhibitors. The exhibition hall, which became known as the Crystal Palace, was covered entirely in glass. The building covered about nineteen acres, and Chance Bros. of Birmingham supplied nearly 900,000 square feet of glazing which weighed about 400 tons. One of the principal features in the centre of the edifice was a large fountain standing twenty-seven feet high, constructed of glass and supported on an iron frame hidden within it which was made by F. & C. Osler of Birmingham. In addition, Thorpe states that there were as many as seventy-nine glass companies exhibiting their products, but that presumably included non-flint glass firms, decorating companies and foreign exhibitors since Powell records only seventeen British glass manufacturers. The list of these included names of companies who became the major innovators and leaders of the industry throughout the next fifty years: Bacchus & Co. of Birmingham; Lloyd & Summerfield, Birmingham; Pellatt & Co., London; Richardson, Stourbridge; Molineaux & Webb, Manchester; James Powell & Co., London.

Among the foreign exhibitors were Harrach of Bohemia showing overlay and coloured glass, Hoffman of Prague showing opaline glass and Neffen of Austria, similar to Hoffman. All these products were subsequently copied in the British Isles.

Because of the great diversity of glass which was made during the second half of the nineteenth century and the

117 The glass fountain built for the Great Exhibition of 1851 by F. & C. Osler.

copying and overlapping between one company and another it is not easy to plot the progress of glassmaking during this period in an orderly and coherent manner. In an effort to provide the interested collector with a framework on which to hang this bewildering variety I have arranged the opposite chart showing the principal and best-known firms with the bare facts of what is known about them. (The entries are grouped by town of operation, and the firms appear alphabetically within each sub-group.) This chart is followed by notes on each one, elaborating the chart. Finally I will review the principal types of glass which they made.

118 A glass plate with sulphide encrustation marked on the back, *c.* 1840. This piece was manufactured by Pellatt & Green, who formerly had been Apsley Pellatt & Co.

Apsley Pellatt & Co., Falcon Works, Southwark, London Apsley Pellatt Senior took over the Falcon Glassworks in Southwark about 1790 and was succeeded in about 1820 by his son Apsley Pellatt Junior. For a while the firm operated as Pellatt & Green but subsequently became Apsley Pellatt & Co., Pellatt Junior retired in 1852 on becoming a Member of Parliament, and the firm continued variously under the control of other members of the family until 1895. Apsley Pellatt Junior was of an enquiring turn of mind, published several books, of which *The Curiosities of Glassmaking*, 1849, is the best known, and patented several new glassmaking techniques. He was best known for the incorporation of small relief-moulded plaques into crystal glass vessels which are commonly called sulphides. I have seen one of these set in a glass plate marked 'Pellatt & Green, Falcon Works, London': the only other mark I know of is on an engraved goblet made for the 1862 Exhibition marked 'Pellatt'. The cut glass which this company produced at the time of the Great Exhibition was of a brilliant whiteness and clarity, with cutting of a very high standard, but generally over-elaborate.

James Powell, Whitefriars Glassworks, London The glasshouse at Whitefriars in London had existed from about 1700 and, as was the case with many glasshouses, had had a succession of owners over the years until it was acquired by James Powell & Sons in 1835. The Powells had come from Bristol where glassmaking was on the decline and they continued in London until 1923 when they moved to Wealdstone so that they could claim to be the last of the London flint glasshouses, which had numbered about fifteen in 1760.

They also showed cut and engraved glass in 1851, but later in the century worked closely with members of the Arts and Crafts Movement.

Powells also made many copies of earlier styles, particularly Venetian and English baluster types. In the 1920's they made

Name	Town	Operating period	Trademark	Principal products
Apsley Pellatt & Co.	London	1820-95	Pellat & Green, Falcon Works, London	Fine cut glass, sulphide encrustation
James Powell	London	1835-1980		Cut glass, copies of antique styles, Arts & Crafts Movement styles
George Bacchus	Birmingham	1818-97	George Bacchus & Son	Coloured glass, transfer prints
Lloyd & Summerfield	Birmingham	1780-?		Glass busts, coloured glass for church windows
F. & C. Osler	Birmingham	1807-?		Cut glass, glass busts, monumental and large glass
Rice Harris & Co.	Birmingham	1830?-60+	I.G.W.	Paperweight, pressed glass
Boulton & Mills	Stourbridge	1876-1925		Coloured, applied foliage, epergnes
W. H., B. & J. Richardson	Stourbridge	1837-1937	Richardson Vitrified	Cut glass, coloured glass, overlay, Etruscan style, painted, transfer
Thomas Webb	Stourbridge	1856-today	Thos. Webb & Sons	Satin glass, Burmese, cameo, coloured, engraved, gilded
Stevens & Williams	Stourbridge	1847-today		Rock crystal engraving, threading, coloured, overlay
Birtles Tate & Co.	Manchester	1858-1922+		Pressed glass, coloured glass
J. Derbyshire & Co.	Manchester	1873-?	JD superimposed on an anchor	Pressed glass, translucent colours, cast animal figures
Molineaux Webb & Co.	Manchester	1825?-1900+		Cut table glass, pressed glass
Percival Vickers	Manchester			Pressed glass
G. Davidson	Gateshead	1867-today	Lion from mural crown	Pressed glass (slag) coloured
Sowerby	Gateshead	1850-today	Peacock head	Pressed glass (slag) coloured
H. Greener & Co.	Sunderland	1869-today	Lion with star or axe	Pressed glass (slag)
W. H. Heppell	Newcastle	1850+-84		Pressed glass (slag)
J. Ford	Edinburgh	1815-1904	Thistle?	Cut glass, pressed glass, engraved glass
J. Couper & Co.	Glasgow	1853-1913	Clutha	Decorative bubbly glass

some reconstructions of fifteenth century glasses based on fragments found in the Chiddingfold area.

George Bacchus, Birmingham This firm exhibited cut overlay glass in the style of Bohemian glass at the 1851 Exhibition. They also produced delicate black transfer prints in the Etruscan style on white opaline glass. They later went on to make pressed glass.

Lloyd & Summerfield, Birmingham Heath This firm exhibited in London both in 1851 and in 1862. At the former exhibition their display included very ornate jugs in coloured overlay glass with applied bunches of grapes in glass, also elaborately engraved wine glasses with serpentine stems in the Venetian style. They are probably best known to collectors, however, for the busts they produced in cast glass with a frosted finish of notable people of the day. Among these were Queen Victoria, Prince Albert and John Wesley.

F. & C. Osler, Broad Street, Birmingham The main claim to fame of this firm seems to have been the outsize examples of cut glass fabrications they produced for the 1851 Exhibition. These included a twenty-foot chandelier as well as the fountain already referred to, which weighed nearly four tons. It is illustrated on p. 125. They also produced glass busts similar to those of Lloyd & Summerfield.

Rice Harris & Co., Islington Glassworks, Birmingham The Art Journal catalogue of the Great Exhibition devoted two pages to the display of Rice Harris, which consisted of extremely elaborate and over-decorated examples of decorative glassware, most of which has a pseudo Bohemian Moorish appearance. Such was the love of ornament at that time that the writer in the Art Journal says: 'The space we have devoted to illustrating a portion of them is not greater than their excellence demands'. The display consisted of 'Ornamental glass of various colours, gilt and enamelled, cut and engraved, consisting of tazzas, compotiers, liqueur services, toilet bottles, claret jugs, vases, specimens of colour combined by casing or coating, specimens of threaded or Venetian glass.'

At the same time they were showing pressed and moulded tumblers, goblets and wine glasses. This was a fairly new art at that time, and Rice Harris must have been among the pioneers of the technique in the Midlands, since they were the only firm recorded as exhibiting these products.

The mark I.G.W. appears in one or two millefiori paperweights and is always taken to refer to the Islington Glass Works.

Boulton & Mills, Audnam Glassworks, Wordsley, Stourbridge This firm made coloured decorative glass, much of it decorated with applied pincered trails of foliage and fruit in coloured glass. They were also leaders in the design and manufacture of épergnes and table centrepieces, without which no Victorian home was complete. These were composed of branches forming flower holders, and arms for hanging baskets.

W. H., B. and J. Richardson, Wordsley, Stourbridge The initials refer to three brothers, William Hayden, Benjamin and Jonathan. The first two worked at the Wordsley Glass Works, which had been in operation since about 1720. In 1829, in conjunction with Thomas Webb, they acquired these works and set up as Webb & Richardson. In 1836 Webb left them, whereupon they were joined by their brother Jonathan to form the company of W. H., B and J. Richardson. This proved to be one of the most adventurous and innovative of all the Midlands glassworks. Benjamin was the most renowned of the three, and under his leadership the firm developed many new styles of colouring and decorating. At the Great Exhibition they showed some of the most florid and heavily cut glass that anyone had ever seen, but by the 1860's they had turned to coloured glass decorated with transfers or coloured enamels in a much more natural style.

They also favoured the Etruscan style which George Bacchus produced, although their wares were more colourful. Another motif they used was the application of handles or ropes of glass to the outside of opaline vessels, which were gilded to look like snakes.

My own personal favourite among their products is a series of water sets which were very realistically painted with water plants—marsh marigolds and yellow irises among them. These patterns were also engraved upon jug and tumbler sets. Their mark is usually Richardson on a banner, with the word 'Vitrified' underneath. The firm survived under the name of Richardson until 1937.

Thomas Webb, Stourbridge This is probably the best known of all the Midlands glass companies, surviving down to the present day under various names, but currently operating as Dema Glass Ltd.

Thomas Webb (1802-69) inherited the White House Glass Works at Wordsley from his father in 1836, which was the reason for his leaving the firm of Webb & Richardson already referred to. After one year he acquired the Platts Glasshouse at Amblecote which had then been making glass for over a hundred years. He continued there until 1855 when he built the new Dennis Glass Works at Amblecote. This became the Webb's Crystal Glass Company in 1919 and in 1964 became part of the Dema Group which includes the old Edinburgh & Leith Flint Glass Company.

At the 1851 Exhibition Thomas Webb & Co. showed table glass, but the Art Journal did not think it important enough to illustrate. However, during the later years of the century they employed some fine engravers, including Fritsche and Kny, and made Burmese glass under licence from the Mount Washington Glass Co. in Boston, U.S.A. They produced cameo glass, which has become so desirable today, satin glass and several other attractive styles with names like 'coraline', 'Peachbloom', 'Alexandrite'. In 1882 they persuaded Jules Barbe, a French gilder, to set up a workshop on their premises and he was responsible for some superb gilding for Webb.

Stevens & Williams, Brierley Hill, Stourbridge This glasshouse arose from the marriage of William Stevens and Samuel Williams to the two daughters of Joseph Silvers, who operated the Moor Lane Glass House in Brierley Hill, the glasshouse having started in about 1779. They changed the name to Stevens & Williams in 1847 and it continues in production at the present time.

They do not appear to have exhibited at the major exhibitions of the period, but were responsible for some good quality and imaginative coloured decorative wares. One of their more striking products was called 'Silveria'; glass vessels of double thickness enclosing a layer of silver leaf and with random threads of coloured glass trailed on the outside. They also manufactured a pinkish-red glass coloured with gold, which contained pockets of air which shine golden as the article is turned. The outside is entirely covered with a fine thread of trailed glass. They had German engravers working for them producing glass engraved in the 'rock crystal' style. Probably the most famous glassmaker and designer to work for them was Frederick Carder who went to America in 1903 where he founded the Steuben Glass Works. He was a prolific designer of both cut glass and coloured decorative glass.

Birtles Tate & Co., Oldham Road, Manchester This well-known Manchester firm made a whole range of glassware, including pressed glass, a number of designs for which were registered. They produced one of the many versions of shaded glass which were popular in the 1880's which they called 'Sunrise'. They also made épergnes. The company was working well into this century.

119 A typical mark of a glassmaker, in this case that of J. Derbyshire & Co.

J. Derbyshire & Co., Manchester There were two firms operating under this name. It would seem as if John and James worked together initially in the 1860's as James Derbyshire & Bros. After changing to J. J. & T. Derbyshire they finally separated, James to set up in Hulme as James Derbyshire & Sons, and John Derbyshire to set up the Regent Flint Glass Works in Salford.

The products of John Derbyshire are better known because he used a trade mark and registered some of his designs. His mark consisted of JD superimposed on an anchor. This is a little confusing, since John Davenport of Longport also used the anchor mark on his pottery. In Davenport's case the anchor was used only until 1830; Derbyshire didn't introduce his until the 1870's.

He appears to have been exclusively a pressed glass manufacturer, and amongst his best-known wares are a series of moulded figures, Punch and Judy, Britannia, Queen Victoria. These are distinctive because of the very oily looking shades of translucent green and yellow glass from which they were sometimes made. His copies of the Landseer lions made for the foot of Nelson's Column are also well known.

In 1877 the company changed its name to the Regent Flint Glass Co., so it is possible that John Derbyshire severed his connection with it. This firm continued into this century but little more is known of it or Derbyshire.

Molineaux Webb & Co., Ancoats, Manchester At the 1851

120 A pressed glass sugar basin and cream jug by Molineaux Webb & Co. of Manchester. They carry the registration mark for 1865.

Exhibition this company displayed a variety of cut and coloured glass which compares favourably with the other products of other, perhaps better known, glasshouses. They are much better known to collectors, however, for their pressed glass and it would seem that later in the century these wares accounted for the bulk of their production. Their work can be identified from the many patterns which they registered. These have such a distinctive quality that with a little practice even their unmarked wares can be identified. Crispness of moulding, the weight and liberal use of frosted areas are typical characteristics of Molineaux Webb. Interestingly these qualities are also apparent in the cut wares they made, which seems to indicate that they translated their attitude towards cut glass into their pressed products.

Percival Vickers, Manchester Although this company made a range of glassware by all the normal methods they were among the first to register designs for pressed glass as early as 1847. The firm began life as Percival Yates; Vickers joined them around 1860, and Yates disappeared about 1870 to leave them with the name they are best known by. They were still registering designs in 1883, the last year of the diamond registration mark.

121 A pressed comporte by Percival Vickers of Manchester. It has the registration mark for 1878.

G. Davidson, Team Glassworks, Gateshead This was one of the two great northern glassmaking firms standing equal in importance with Sowerbys. It was founded by George Davidson, a local businessman, in 1867 when one of its principal products was glass chimneys for oil lamps. In 1881 they acquired the stock, moulds and patterns of the Neville Glass Works (the same Samuel Neville who had left Sowerbys in 1874). Then in 1884 they also acquired the moulds and stock of W. H. Heppell & Co. of Newcastle and also those of Thomas Gray & Co. of Gateshead. This gave them a large and varied range of patterns which appeared subsequently in their own pattern books.

It was to prove of great benefit when George's son Thomas Davidson joined the company in the 1870's. He was a man of great imagination and artistic ability, and became responsible for the great majority of the designs produced by the company. There is some similarity between the Davidson 'slag glass' patterns and colours and those of Sowerby, but each firm had its own distinctive style, so that with a little practice it is usually possible to identify unmarked pieces. Davidsons used the mark of a lion emerging from a mural crown, but rarely registered any of their patterns. From looking at surviving catalogues it appears to me that G. Davidson & Co. produced a wider range of patterns and designs, but many of them were for purely utilitarian domestic use. They also continue in production up to the present time making industrial glassware.

Sowerby's Ellison Glassworks, Gateshead Like so many glassworks, this one had a long and varied history before it became known by the name above, and produced the glass for which it is best known.

George Sowerby set up a glasshouse in Pipewellgate, Gateshead in about 1765. It continued in the control of the family, moving to new premises in Ellison Street in 1850. This must have been large by the standards of the day, since it had six 8-pot furnaces.

It was from this time that pressed glass manufacture was started, and Sowerbys went on to become one of the most inventive and innovative in this field in the United Kingdom.

In 1855 John Sowerby took into partnership Samuel Neville, who had learned his craft in Stourbridge, and the firm became Sowerby & Neville. Neville left in 1874 to start his own glasshouse, and for the next eight years the firm was Sowerby & Co. In 1882 another John Sowerby changed the name to Sowerby's Ellison Glass Co. Ltd.

By 1887 the company had offices in the major capitals of

Europe, much of their production was exported, and they were employing up to 1000 men.

When the registration of trade marks was introduced, Sowerbys were among the first to register, using a peacock's head mark which was the family crest of a branch of the Sowerby family. Much of their production bore this mark and the registration mark, thus making it attractive to collectors today since it can be readily identified.

They are best known for that type of pressed glass which is commonly called slag glass today, but which they called vitro-porcelain. It was opaque coloured glass pressed into a wide variety of attractive shapes and patterns. At the height of its popularity Sowerbys were producing 150 tons per week of finished products. The company survives today making industrial glassware.

H. Greener & Co., Wear Flint Glassworks, Sunderland
Glassmaking in Sunderland goes back to the eighteenth century, and Henry Greener was born into a glassmaking family in 1820. He was apprenticed in Newcastle, and for a time worked for Sowerbys.

In 1858 he formed a partnership with James Angus and operated the Wear Flint Glass Works as Angus & Greener. In 1869 Angus died, and Greener then built a new glasshouse at Millfield. When Henry Greener died in 1882 he instructed his executors, members of the family, to continue the business in the same way under the same name. Apparently this was not a good idea, since in 1885 the business was taken over by James Jobling, a Newcastle chemical merchant. The name was changed to Greener & Co., and the company took on a new lease of life, extending its range of domestic and industrial wares. In the 1920's it introduced the first heat-resistant domestic glassware under the name of Pyrex.

H. Greener & Co. was another of the few firms to use a trade mark. Initially this was a demi-lion rampant bearing in its right paw a star. After the business was taken over by Jobling the star was changed for a halberd. Neither Greener mark is common, but the latter mark is much more infrequent than the former. There is sometimes confusion between the Davidson and Greener marks, but the thing to remember is that the Davidson mark is distinguished by the mural crown, which looks like a crenellated turret.

Although Greener used most of the same opaque colours as the other 'slag glass' manufacturers, they have their own style. One popular feature on their jugs and tankards was a handle made with a rustic or wood finish. They also seem to have been

134

quick to issue commemorative items.

W. H. Heppell, Newcastle Flint Glassworks, Newcastle Although this company did not have a very long life it deserves notice because it registered some twelve designs, and its authorship of these can be traced from the registration marks.

William Henry Heppell took over an existing glasshouse in about 1869 and produced some interesting pressed glass until George Davidson acquired the moulds and patterns in 1884. Best known, perhaps, are a series of jugs formed like fish standing upright, the tails folded round to provide the handle and the mouths open to form the rim and pouring lip.

J. Ford, Holyrood Glassworks, Edinburgh This company was started in 1810 by William Ford, who acquired a glass-house which had been in operation since the late eighteenth century. He died in 1819 and the company was taken over by Bailey & Co. of the Midlothian Glass Works, with his nephew, John Ford, being one of the directors. In 1835 the company was dissolved and John Ford took it over on his own account. This was when it became the Holyrood Flint Glass Works. The business expanded and produced a wide range of good quality domestic glassware.

John Ford died in 1865 and the name was changed to John Ford & Co. under the management of William Ford, John's son, and Francis Ranken, a member of another local family of glassmakers. The manufacturing side of the business ended in 1904, although the retail side continued under the Rankens until 1959.

Much of the product was engraved, and the fern leaf decoration, so popular in Victorian times, was one of their most popular subjects. In the 1860's, a Bohemian engraver named Müller came to work in Edinburgh, and over the following years he and his son carried out some excellent work on the glass made by J. Ford & Co. They produced pressed glass in quantity and a thistle mark which very rarely appears on these wares is sometimes attributed to them, but there is no proof of this so far.

J. Couper & Son, City Glassworks, Glasgow This firm is interesting because William Haden Richardson of the Stour-bridge glass family worked for them for a period from 1853. In the 1890's they produced a style of greenish glass inset with bubbles of air which gave it a distinctly antique appearance. This was called 'Clutha', and was designed for them by, among others, Christopher Dresser, well-known in the 'Arts and Crafts' Movement. Some of the patterns drew on Roman and Persian styles for their inspiration.

Chapter 7

Victorian decorative glass

I have already remarked on the difficulty of dating Victorian glass or putting it into any coherent sequence. This is because some styles became popular and enjoyed a long period of popularity (e.g. some styles of decanters) whereas others came and went in a short space of time to be replaced by other styles totally dissimilar. One good generalisation which can be made, however, is that cut glass fell out of favour by the 1860's and did not become popular again until the 1880's. The reaction that set in during the intervening period led to the popularity of thinly blown glassware either made in a free flowing style or decorated in a naturalistic manner.

Because of these extremes of taste it will be easier to discuss Victorian glass under the headings of decoration.

Cut glass

Although I have dealt largely with this subject in chapters two and especially five, there are one or two further points to make with regard to the cut glass of the late Victorian era. As cut glass began to regain its popularity in the 1880's the old shallow cutting of the Georgian period and the deep mitre cutting of the early Victorian era gave way to very elaborate and ornate styles which covered the surface with a multitude of straight lines which produced patterns of stars and diamonds. This can be seen on many of the square decanters of the period which were made in sets of two or three to fill a lockable stand known as a tantalus. In America this type of cutting was known as brilliant cutting, which describes it exactly. In the twentieth century this over-effusive style gave way to patterns of a few deep cuts crossing one another at angles and leaving most of the surface untouched.

Engraved glass

The standard of engraving on glass improved dramatically during the nineteenth century. Some of the finest exponents were artists from Germany and Bohemia who settled in Britain;

122 *Opposite:* A collection of coloured and cased vases, c. 1850. The National Trust, Cotehele House, Calstock.

123 A pair of 'Queen's Ware Burmese glass' vases by Thomas Webb & Co, *c.* 1886, made under licence from the Mount Washington Glass Co. of America. The colouring was obtained by the inclusion of gold and uranium among the ingredients.

Frederick Kny and William Fritsche are probably the best known because they left signed pieces and well documented items which were exhibited at all the major exhibitions. As well as these two, who worked in the Birmingham/Stourbridge area, other Continental names which are recorded include F. Scheibner, J. Schiller and J. Keller. In London Paul Oppitz was a freelance engraver who worked for, among others, Copeland. In Scotland Miller, another Keller, Lerche and Tieze were all European craftsmen who engraved for Edinburgh and Glasgow glasshouses. The last named, Tieze, also worked in Dublin where Joseph Eisert is recorded as an engraver. There was nothing new about this influx, of course. When the demand for cut glass arose in the early eighteenth century, German cutters were introduced into Britain, so the story was repeating itself.

This influx of foreign talent encouraged a rise in the art generally, and a number of native-born engravers rose to great prominence during the second half of the century. W. J. Muckley engraved for Richardsons and exhibited at the Great Exhibition, as did Thomas Wood of Stourbridge. Probably the most important amongst the English decorators was John Northwood. Born in 1836, he learned the art of decorating glass with W. H., B. & J. Richardson, to whom he was apprenticed in 1848. He was a fine artist and studied at the Stourbridge School of Art. In 1859 he set up his own design and decorating workshops, where he was responsible for a number of advances in decorating technique. Among these were 'intaglio' cutting—a method which combined the freedom of engraving with the depth of cutting; the pattern copying machine for acid etching, and most important of all, the art of cameo engraving on glass. In 1882 he joined Stevens & Williams as artistic director, where he remained until his death in 1902. During his life he was at the hub of the glass industry in Stourbridge and was associated with all the leading members of it.

Wheel engraving achieves its effect by the abrasion of the surface over the whole area of the design. Intaglio engraving is more deeply cut into the surface, so that elements of the pattern may be said to be in reverse relief, with the highest points of the pattern being the surface of the glass. The Germans called this 'Tiefschitt' (deep cutting).

A development of this technique led to one of the most distinctive forms of Victorian engraving, the style known as 'rock crystal'. In this the whole surface of the vessel was worked on to produce intaglio designs, usually in panels, which were surrounded by ornamentation. The surface was then highly polished to produce the effect which the Chinese carvers had achieved on blocks of natural crystal, hence its name. Leading exponents of this technique were Kny, Fritzche and an Englishman, John Orchard, who worked for Stevens & Williams. This highly ornate and elaborate style is sometimes mistaken for moulded work, but its very high polish distinguishes it.

Cameo

In its purest form this style is carried out by carving rather than engraving, but over the years the method was modified to include wheel engraving and acid etching.

It owes its development in England to a desire to produce a copy of the famous Portland, or Barberini, vase which Sir William Hamilton brought back from Italy in the eighteenth century. It is a first century Roman vase, about 9 inches high, of dark blue glass overlaid with carved classical scenes in white glass. John Northwood was encouraged to attempt a copy by Benjamin Richardson and Phillip Pargetter, whose glassworks produced the blank which had a layer of white glass over a base of dark blue glass. With carving tools of his own design and manufacture Northwood spent three years from 1873 to 1876 in producing this copy. Unfortunately, when nearing completion it cracked, and Northwood attributed this to stresses induced by the differences in the two layers of glass. After several more years of experimentation he solved this problem and evolved a technique for producing cameo glass with as many as four different layers of colour. As the technique of cutting through these layers developed it became common to remove the surplus metal by grinding or by acid etching, while only the finishing was carried out by carving.

There developed some very able exponents of this method, George and Thomas Woodall being perhaps the most famous after Northwood. The modelling of the designs is achieved by the degree to which the base colour shows through the superimposed layers.

As with so many Victorian styles, the mass demand for expensive objects was met by reproducing them in the crudest and coarsest manner. This was true of cameo glass, and one often finds vases in the typical colours of blue, dark red and amber overlaid with painted white enamel decoration which gives it a superficial impression of cameo work.

Silver coating

The foregoing comments apply equally to a type of glass patented in 1849 by F. Hale Thompson and Edward Varnish.

140

This was made in a manner similar to the silvered container in a vacuum flask today, in that a solution of silver was deposited on the interior of a double walled vessel, which was then sealed to protect the coating. This was then often covered with a layer of transparent coloured glass, and through this a pattern was cut to expose the bright silver finish beneath. Genuine pieces are of noticeably good quality and set into the base is a disc bearing the words 'Hale Thompson's Patent, London', 'E. Varnish & Co. Patent, London' or, much more rarely 'W. Lund, Patent, London'. These wares were obviously very popular since one sees, even today, many badly made copies of extremely light weight, with no seal in the bottom and usually with crudely applied enamel decoration.

Enamelled wares

I have already referred to the beautiful enamelled wares of Richardsons, which they produced in the 1860's, but the enamelled decoration with which most people are more familiar is that known as 'Mary Gregory'. It takes its name from a lady who worked as a decorator for the Boston & Sandwich Glass Co. in America during the 1870's and 1880's. There has been some controversy over the years as to whether she actually existed, but in a book on the subject by R. W. Miller published in the U.S.A. in 1972 there are two photographs of her. She lived from 1856-1908.

The subjects she is most associated with are the figures of boys and girls, usually in some form of floral landscape. These are mostly in white enamel, but in the last years of the nineteenth century coloured enamels were used for the hands and feet.

These pieces achieved considerable popularity in Britain, but it is difficult to establish which examples may have been imported from America and which, if any, were decorated here. The style was extensively copied in Bohemia and Austria and from the very varying quality of the examples I see, I think most of what appears on the British market came from Europe. Collectors of this type of ware should be wary, as they are being copied today, both in America and in England. In the same style are many coloured jugs with floral decoration on them, usually lily of the valley. These certainly came from Europe.

Venetian and 'aesthetic' glass

The reaction against cut glass and heavy white crystal that set in during the decade from 1850 was encouraged both by the leaders of fashion and by several exhibitions of old Venetian glass which caught the public imagination. John Ruskin in *The Stones of Venice* declared that 'all cut glass is barbarous' and made a plea for glass that was an expression of artistic freedom rather than mechanical formality. This trend coincided with a revival of glassmaking in Venice itself and from 1862 onwards modern Venetian made reproductions of antique patterns were exhibited at all the major European exhibitions.

This revival of interest in Venetian glass meant that the wheel of fashion had gone round full circle, and the art from which English glassmaking of the eighteenth century had sprung once again found favour. The Venetian style was expressed in two ways by British glassmakers; some of them including James Powell & Son at the Whitefriars Glassworks and Jenkinson in Edinburgh produced faithful copies of the originals, while others used the patterns of Venice as a springboard from which to develop their own ideas. This revival gradually evolved in two directions; the first leading to the glassware of the Arts and Crafts Movement during the 1860's and 1870's, the second to the multitude of decorative coloured patterns of the last twenty-five years of the century. The former may be seen as the intellectual expression in glassmaking, while the latter, catering for a mass market, was its popular demonstration.

Venetian glass, with its thinly blown elaborate shapes, was a glassblower's art rather than a decorator's art. So in returning to this style the glassmakers were once again given an opportunity to express themselves as they had not done for many years. All the decorative devices of the Venetians were rediscovered. The diamond pattern produced by drawing together trailed threads of glass which Ravenscroft referred to as 'nipt diamond waies' they recreated as a diamond moulded pattern. This in turn led to a method of trapping pockets of air between two layers of glass which became popular as satin glass. The serpentine stems of Venetian wine glasses were copied; hollow blown knopped stems and pincered trails found favour and for a few years Venice became the most important single influence. The use of colour became widespread, not only as plain colours but also as mixtures of colours on the same object. The Venetians applied blobs of different coloured glass to the outside of a vessel, but the Victorians incorporated reds, yellows, greens and blues into the body of the vessel. This type of ware is often called 'end of day' glass, suggesting that these colours were the scraps left over which were casually incorporated into glass vessels. This is not true, since there are so many of them, even today, that they must have been in regular production.

Alexander Jenkinson in Edinburgh produced some very good copies in the 1870's, particularly those with 'latticinio' decoration. This was the pattern of fine white threads sometimes straight, sometimes twisted, which spread through the whole article. It was from this technique that the opaque twist stems of the eighteenth century had derived.

One of the leaders of the Arts and Crafts Movement was William Morris, and he was instrumental in encouraging a new aesthetic approach to design amongst the leading artists and craftsmen of his day. Although, with Ruskin and others, he was an advocate of the idea of freedom of expression for creative minds, the glassware that was produced under his patronage was much plainer than the Venetian glass of the day. The first designs he commissioned were those by Phillip Webb in about 1860, and Webb then went on to produce a series of designs which were made by James Powell & Sons and sold by Morris & Co. These were thinly blown glasses on slender stems almost free of adornment. They depended on outline and proportion rather than decoration for their appeal.

Powells also commissioned designs from T. G. Jackson, an architect and designer who was also a member of the Arts Movement. They continued to be associated with the artistic movements of the last part of the century, including Art Nouveau and under the direction of H. J. Powell (1853-1922) experimented with ideas drawn from the past as well as the present so that much of Powell's work remained distinctively different from the mainstream of later Victorian glassmaking.

The 'aesthetic' designers were not afraid to draw their inspiration from any period that they considered acceptable, and their products sometimes showed the effect of a mixture of sources. At the end of the nineteenth century Powells produced wine glasses which captured the spirit of English baluster glasses, but in combinations which never occurred in the eighteenth century. Another source of inspiration was Roman glass and James Couper of Glasgow produced a range of designs in the 1890's created for them by Christopher Dresser and George Walton, which they called 'Clutha'. These were made in a greenish glass shot through with air bubbles in vaguely antique shapes to imitate Roman glass both in texture and shape. This name should not be confused with 'Cluthra', another name found occasionally on glass, but which was made by Frederick Carder at the Steuben Glass Works in America in about 1930.

In the late 1880's cut glass started to regain its popularity and the Arts and Crafts Movement declined. However, the general taste for coloured decorative glass was well established, and this side of the industry continued to flourish.

The major manufacturers vied with each other to produce new colours, and articles in which colours changed gradually with no visible line of separation were popular. This effect was achieved by including some chemical in the composition of the glass which caused a change of colour when part of the vessel was reheated. The best known of these is Burmese glass. First introduced in 1885 by the Mount Washington Glass Co. in America it was made here by Thomas Webb as Queens Ware Burmese. This glass contained uranium which produced, in the first instance, an opaque yellow colour and when this was partly reheated the glass shaded to a bright pink. Other versions produced by other companies went under the names of 'Amberina' (amber to ruby), 'Alexandrite' (purplish red to blue) and 'Sunrise' (similar to Burmese).

Glassware decorated with iridescent colours became popular in the last years of the century. The idea originated on the Continent, and examples appeared at several international exhibitions. The firms of Lobmeyr and Loetz in Austria were specialists in this type of decoration, and Thomas Webb & Sons appear to have been the first company to produce it in England, having taken out a patent for it in 1878. The effect was achieved by coating the glass with a film of metallic salts which, when heated, became iridescent.

The Venetian aspects which survived, usually in an exaggerated form, included frilled edges to vases and bowls, which were produced with crimping tongs, and ribbed handles and prunts. The handles had fine ribs running along their length which produced a multi-pointed star effect where they joined the body of the vessel. When the ribbed pattern was used on prunts it produced an effect like a scallop shell.

A useful way to judge the period of any glass vessel with a handle is from the way in which the handle is applied. As a general rule, up to 1860 handles were added by applying a lump of glass to the rim of the vessel, which was then drawn out and the end crimped on to the body. After this date the general practice was reversed, with the glass being applied to the body, drawn up, and the end turned in before it was applied to the rim. The result is that the handle generally tapers from the point at which it is applied to the point where the free end is attached. Exceptions to this rule are the small round-bodied custard glasses of the late nineteenth century which

124 *Above:* A heavy bowl engraved with alternate panels of dragons and flowers in the 'rock crystal' style. It is signed on the shoulder FRITCHIE, which is probably a corruption of (William) Fritsche. Fritsche was a famous exponent of this style of engraving, and in the Stourbridge area his name was commonly used in the manner found on this bowl. Miss A. Carwardine.

125 *Right:* A wheel-engraved water jug showing a cottage scene, dated 1860. Pilkington Glass Museum, St Helens.

"IVORINE" BASKETS AND FLOWER HOLDERS.

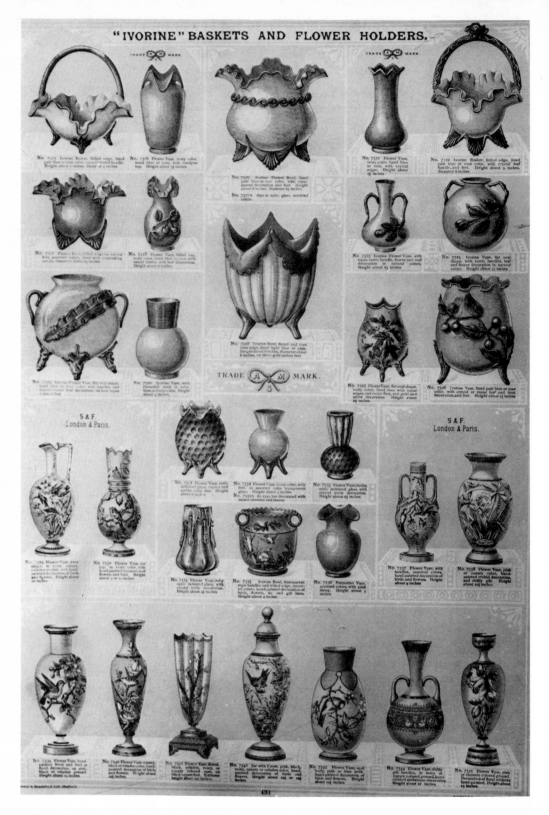

126 *Opposite:* A page from a late nineteenth century catalogue showing a variety of the coloured and decorated vases so popular at that period.

127 *Right:* A small vase that combines the revival of the Venetian taste with the fashion for iridescent glass. The iridescent bronze-green body has applied shell prunts studded with coloured glass jewels. It was possibly manufactured by Stevens & Williams, *c.* 1880. Miss A. Cawardine.

128 *Below:* A vase by Thomas Webb & Son. The enamel and gilt decoration is signed by Jules Barbe, a French decorator who had a studio at the Webb factory from 1882 to 1920.

129 *Above:* A pair of small white jugs with hand-painted floral decoration in the manner of Thomas Bott, who worked for Richardson's of Stourbridge, *c.* 1860.

130 *Left:* As with **127**, another example of the Venetian revival, but with a strong English flavour to it. The red body has an applied trailed thread overlaid with prunts and vertical lines of clear glass, *c.* 1880.

131 *Above:* A group of items from the Sowerby's Ellison Glassworks at Gateshead, all *c.* 1880. The back four pieces are press moulded and carry the Sowerby peacock head trademark. The pattern was occasionally picked out in colour as in the example on the extreme right. The piece in the foreground is an example of their hand-blown Venetian style, and is similar to one of their pressed patterns. Miss A. Cawardine.

132 *Right:* A vase composed of a type of glass popular from the 1860's onward. The translucent yellow body has a raised moulded pattern which shades to an opalescent white. This type of glass was widely used for lamp and light fittings. Miss A. Cawardine.

usually have handles applied in the earlier method.

Satin glass which I mentioned earlier, was made by several firms. The usual method was to blow opaque white glass into a mould to produce a diamond pattern. When this was cased with a layer of coloured glass, usually red or blue, a series of air pockets were formed between the two layers. The satin finish was achieved by etching the finished vessel in acid. The practice of coating a base layer of opaque glass with various colours of translucent glass was widespread and popular.

The coloured decorative glass of the last quarter of the nineteenth century was produced in such profusion that it inevitably varies widely in quality. Unfortunately it is generally judged by the standard of the worst, but there is much that is worth a closer look, for the best is very good, and it will

136, 137 The two ways handles were fixed in the nineteenth century. (Top) This method was used mainly before 1860. (Bottom) This method was used mainly after 1860.

certainly attract more attention as time passes. Remember that popular taste changes, and one should try to judge this type of glass as our forefathers did. It may be largely out of favour at the moment, but it has a vitality and exuberance that will surely make it collectable in the future.

Pressed glass

The production of glass objects by the moulding method is as old as the material itself, but during the nineteenth century the process was improved by the development of a technique whereby the glass was forced into a mould under pressure. This meant that the shapes produced and the decorative effects achieved were limited only by the imagination of the designer and the ability of the mould makers. The equipment consisted of a mould and a punch. The mould, which was normally made in two, three or four sections, carried the pattern for the outside of the article, while the punch was shaped to the profile of the interior. When the punch was lowered into the mould the two met to form an enclosed space of a fixed volume. The process required a measured amount of molten glass of this volume to be placed in the mould, and when the punch was brought down the glass was forced out into the shape of the

138 *Opposite:* A page of pressed glass patterns from a catalogue of 1885. It includes items by George Davidson and Sowerby.

No. 7806 Oval Dish, pressed glass, made in five sizes; length,
6 inches, 7½ inches, 9 inches, 10½ inches, and 12 inches
Round Dish, to match, in five sizes; diameter, 5 inches, 6 inches,
7½ inches, 9 inches, 10½ inches, and 12 inches

No. 7805 Butter Dish and Cover, pressed
glass, diameter about 6 inches

No. 7807 Butter Dish and Cover, pressed
glass, diameter about 6½ inches

No. 7809 Oval Dish, plain, clear glass, notched edge, star bottom,
made in seven sizes; length, 5 inches, 6 inches, 7 inches, 8 inches,
9 inches, 10 inches, and 11 inches
Round Dish, to match, in seven sizes; diameter, 5 inches, 6 inches,
7 inches, 8 inches, 9 inches, 10 inches, and 11 inches

No. 7808 Butter Dish and Cover, cut one
row hollows, diameter about 6½ inches

No. 7810 Butter Dish and Cover, engraved,
diameter about 6½ inches

No. 7812 Oval Dish, pressed glass, made in five sizes; length,
6 inches, 7½ inches, 9 inches, 10½ inches, and 12 inches

No. 7811 Butter Dish and Cover, pressed iced
glass, extreme width about 8 inches

No. 7813 Butter Dish and Cover, pressed
glass, diameter about 7½ inches

S&F London.

S&F London.

No. 7815 Oval Dish, pressed glass, made in four sizes; length,
6½ inches, 7½ inches, 9 inches, and 10½ inches
Round Dish, to match, made in five sizes; diameter, 5 inches,
6½ inches, 8½ inches, 9½ inches, and 10½ inches

No. 7814 Butter Dish and Cover, frosted ground,
cut stars, diameter about 7 inches

No. 7816 Butter Dish and Cover, oval,
perforated edge, pressed glass, length about 7 in.

No. 7818 Oval Dish, pressed glass, made in seven sizes; length,
6 inches, 7 inches, 8 inches, 9 inches, 10 inches, 11 inches, and
12 inches
Round Dish, to match, made in eight sizes; 5 inches, 6 inches,
7 inches, 8 inches, 9 inches, 10 inches, 11 inches, and 12 inches

TRADE MARK

No. 7817 Butter Dish and Cover, pressed
glass, diameter about 6½ inches

No. 7819 Butter Dish and Cover, pressed
glass, diameter about 7 inches

mould. If the quantity of glass was less than the space between punch and mould there would be holes or gaps in the finished article. If there was too much glass the excess would overflow the mould and prevent the punch making contact with it. Since the punch has to be withdrawn from the glass vessel when it is formed it must be tapered so that the end which forms the bottom of the interior is narrower than the root which coincides with the mouth of the vessel. With flat objects such as plates this problem does not arise.

The introduction of press moulding produced a number of advantages for the glassmaker. It obviated the need for skilled glass blowers (which was not well received); it enabled cheap versions of expensive items like cut glass to be mass produced; the mass production enabled the manufacturers to reach a wider market, and the decorative possibilities offered by this method of manufacture were far greater than could be achieved by any other method.

I often meet people who talk of pressed glass in disparaging terms, and I think this arises from their experience of the mass produced copies of cut glass patterns. The difference in quality is generally so noticeable that it can only compare unfavourably with the real thing. When the technique was used to exploit the full potential of press moulding the products were

139 Two pressed tankards. The first is an unusual pictorial piece by George Davidson; the second is an imitation cut glass tankard marked on the base with a thistle.

140 An unusual pressed celery vase. It appears that the decoration on the body has been highlighted by polishing the pattern and that the obscured surface finish has been achieved manually. There is a registration mark for 1868.

distinctive, owed nothing to any other method, and were often very attractive.

Press moulding, as a mechanical method of glass production, was first developed in the United States. The first patents were taken out in about 1830 and during the succeeding years the American manufacturers were quick to develop and exploit the process until it became an entirely mechanical one.

It found its way across the Atlantic during the 1830's and Apsley Pellatt in *The Curiosities of Glass Making* illustrates an early hand-operated press for making moulded glass. It is not easy to identify early examples of press moulded glass, but there are examples which commemorate the coronation of Queen Victoria in 1837 and her marriage to Prince Albert in 1840. For the most part they were probably used for utilitarian wares such as tumblers. The first patterns to be registered were those of Rice Harris in 1840; from then on patterns were registered regularly, mostly by firms in Stourbridge and Manchester. The first of the northern glassmakers to register a design seems to have been Angus & Greener of Sunderland in 1858. This firm registered their designs regularly from then on, but it is not until 1872 that Sowerbys first registered any designs for pressed glass. Sowerbys gradually increased the number of patterns they registered until by 1877 they were registering more than all other firms put together.

If a registration mark is found on a piece of glass, it is a useful guide to the age of the piece. From 1842 it was possible to protect new patterns and designs by registering them at the registry office. These patterns may be identified by the diamond registration marks which, in the case of pressed glass, were incorporated in the mould and appear somewhere on the surface of the finished article. The registration mark consisted of a diamond divided into five parts with a partially hidden circle at its apex. The Roman numeral in the circle referred to the class of manufacture (III meant glass), the internal segments of the diamond showed the date the patent was registered and by which manufacturer. The following chart gives the sequence of code letters for the months and years, which will enable the exact date of registration to be identified. The presence of a registration mark on any object does not guarantee that it was made at that date. The design protection lasted four years and after that the mark no longer had any significance but would continue to appear as long as the mould bearing it remained in use.

The letters of the alphabet were used in a random sequence for the first twenty-six years after which the order was

1842-1867	Years		Months	
	1842–X	1855–E	January	–C
	1843–H	1856–L	February	–G
	1844–C	1857–K	March	–W
	1845–A	1858–B	April	–H
	1846–I	1859–M	May	–E
	1847–F	1860–Z	June	–M
	1848–U	1861–R	July	–I
	1849–S	1862–O	August	–R
	1850–V	1863–G	September	–D
	1851–P	1864–N	October	–B
	1852–D	1865–W	November	–K
	1853–Y	1866–Q	December	–A
	1854–J	1867–T		

(R may be found as the month mark for 1-19 September 1857, and K for December 1860.)

1868-1883	Years		Months	
	1868–X	1876–V	January	–C
	1869–H	1877–P	February	–G
	1870–C	1878–D	March	–W
	1871–A	1879–Y	April	–H
	1872–I	1880–J	May	–E
	1873–F	1881–E	June	–M
	1874–U	1882–L	July	–I
	1875–S	1883–K	August	–R
			September	–D
			October	–B
			November	–K
			December	–A

(For 1-6 March 1878, G was used for the month and W for the year.)

repeated, but in a different division of the diamond. In 1884 these marks were abandoned and replaced by the more familiar registered numbers.

Surviving catalogues of pressed glass issued by George Davidson, John Ford and some of the Stourbridge manufacturers show pages of designs for utilitarian tableware in clear glass. It was the firms of the north-east who developed the decorative or fancy side of the trade by introducing ornamental wares in a variety of opaque colours. Sowerby's catalogues for 1879 and 1882 have survived, and these are entirely devoted to ornamental and decorative wares in such colours as white, black, turquoise, malachite, green, a cream colour they called Ivory Queens Ware, in imitation of cream-ware pottery, and an opalescent colour called 'blanc de lait'. The colours they are best known for today, however, is a marbled purple and white. There were other marbled colours, blue and white and green and white, but none of these were exclusive to Sowerby. Davidson, Greener and Heppell all

141 *Opposite:* A page from the Art Journal catalogue of the Great Exhibition of 1851, showing some of the display of Richardsons' of Stourbridge. Note the elaborate and heavy cutting on many of the pieces.

novel in style and rich in colour; of these we shall engrave specimens. The two DECANTERS with which we commence our illustrations, are of the purest crystal; the lozenge-shape cuttings bring out the prismatic colours with exceeding brilliancy: the GOBLET at the head of the second column is elegant in form, and the introduction of the vine upon the cup,

of the cutting, while it retains all its boldness. The next subject is a BUTTER DISH of crystal, designed after the style of the antique. The VASE that follows is very elegant; it is manufactured in opal; the scroll and band at top and bottom are gilt; the flowers and fruit painted with vitrified

enamel colours. The DECANTER completing that page is most lustrous, and the lozenge-shaped cutting exceedingly bold. All the objects introduced in this page are of crystal of the purest kind; the beauty and variety of the cutting in the

though not a novelty, is appropriate. The FRUIT DISH and STAND that follows is of ruby glass covered on flint, and then cut through, showing the two colours to great advantage. The WINE GLASS is very elaborately ornamented, and the stem, which looks a little heavy in the engraving, loses this appearance in the original object, by the style

whole of these works cannot fail to secure to them unqualified admiration. The large group at the bottom consists of one of each articles in a set of glass for dessert purposes, consequently they are all of a similar pattern, except the CLARET JUG, which is cut in a similar style, but is somewhat varied in its decoration.

157

142 *Left:* A moulded celery vase bearing the mark of George Davidson, *c.* 1885. Miss A. Carwardine.

143 *Opposite:* A Richardson's water jug and goblet in white glass with enamelled decoration of reedmace, *c.* 1880. The firm produced other fine sets decorated with water plants such as marsh marigold and yellow iris. These patterns may also be sometimes found engraved on clear glass.

produced articles in these combinations. One useful point of identification, when trade marks are absent, is that George Davidson frequently used a series of concentric moulded rings on the underside of their products.

The peacock's head was Sowerby's trade mark, and they also used the peacock motif on a number of their products in the form of a decorative border. They also produced a whole series of posy vases of different shapes, each bearing a pattern derived from a nursery rhyme. The commonest of these are Old King Cole and Oranges and Lemons, but others such as Mary Mary Quite Contrary and Little Jack Horner are quite rare. Some examples are embellished with gilding over the figures, while some of the jug and basin sets have the floral patterns

144 *Opposite:* A pair of tall glass vases manufactured to represent palm trees. This is Stourbridge work of the 1880's. Miss A. Cawardine.

145 *Above:* A collection of Victorian drinking glasses. Private Collection.

146 *Right:* Three pressed jugs. The outer ones are by George Davidson. The central one is unmarked but probably dates from about 1850 since the handle has been applied by hand.

hand painted in coloured enamels. Sowerby also introduced a series of translucent colours which included red, lime green and ice blue.

Although the Sowerby pattern books are concerned principally with press moulded articles, they contain a few patterns which could only be achieved by blow moulding. In this technique the shape is produced by air pressure, usually from the glass blower's lungs, and they are easily recognised because the narrowest part of the body is at the neck, and the pattern is never as distinct as on press moulded items.

The popularity of these coloured pressed wares lasted for about fifteen years from 1875, but gradually the taste for cut glass reasserted itself and the geometric pattern took over from the naturalistic design.

As explained earlier, G. Davidson acquired the patterns of several other firms, but of their own designs some of the most distinctive and attractive are a range of wares covered in a marine design consisting of coral and shells. Davidson's most distinctive product, however, was their 'Pearline' glass. This was translucent blue or yellow fading to opaque white at the rim or edge, which they introduced in 1889. This shading was achieved by reheating the object after it was pressed, whereupon the high spots or edges turned opaque.

The only colours used by the Manchester pressed glass makers seem to have been translucent shades of green, yellow and a dark purple which appears black until a strong light is shone through it. Otherwise they confined themselves to domestic articles like jugs, basins, celery vases, comports, plates, tumblers and so on. Colin Lattimore's book on pressed glass gives a list of registration marks for pressed glass and the firms who registered them. By reference to this, and with a little practice the individual style of each firm becomes recognisable so that even unmarked pieces may be attributed to their manufacturer.

Occasionally one may find marked pieces of pressed glass which bear marks that do not relate to any of those I have mentioned. It is most likely that these are of American origin, and the marks that I see most frequently are a capital *C* within a triangle for the Cambridge (Ohio) Glass Company; *I. G.* for the Imperial Glass Company and *W. G.* for the Westmorland Glass Company. These last two marks are usually on modern reproductions of old patterns.

As a collectable commodity pressed glass is just beginning to attract the attention it deserves and I am sure that during the next few years we are going to see a rapidly increasing interest in what was, after all, one of the major nineteenth century contributions to glassmaking.

147 A double-walled and silvered inkwell marked 'W. Lund, London', *c*. 1850.

Chapter 8

Copies and fakes

I regularly meet people who are totally unaware of the diversity and quality of antique glassware. After the initial reaction of surprise the next question is invariably 'How can one tell that it is genuine and not a later copy?'. This is undoubtedly prompted by the fact that they see a strong similarity in the metal of two hundred and fifty years ago with that of the glassware which graces our tables today. This problem is made more difficult to resolve since glass, given reasonable care, does not deteriorate with age. I have seen pieces of Roman glass of such clarity that they look as if they had just come from the glasshouse. Most other materials that man uses to manufacture his domestic and utilitarian objects show the effects of use and wear. Wood discolours with age, or acquires a patina with constant polishing, fabrics fray and become threadbare, metals also acquire a patina or wear at the edges. Glass, on the other hand, retains its lustre and its clarity unimpaired by age. It was either broken and disposed of, or it survives to stand comparison with the best that modern glassmakers can produce.

As much for its enduring appeal as for probably any other reason, glassware has been copied down the ages, and the ability to distinguish these copies from the originals is to some extent a matter of experience. After looking for long enough at any type of object I am sure that one acquires an instinctive feel for what is right or wrong. Sometimes this is apparent even before a close examination reveals the tell-tale signs of the copy. It is a question of proportion, balance, style and character. These are the things that are almost impossible to put into words, but there are a number of more specific details that one may look for to decide whether a glass is genuine or not.

The words copy, reproduction and fake are commonly used indiscriminately to signify anything meant to deceive, but this is not necessarily so. Copies are usually limited numbers of an article individually made, and not always exact imitations. Modern limited edition paperweights are an example of this.

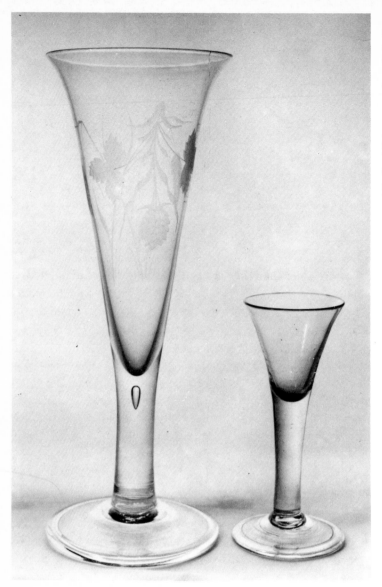

The styles of the much sought after French weights of the 1850's are copied, but the modern ones usually contain a date cane to show that they have merit in their own right. A common sight in some art galleries is the person copying a famous painting. These are either intended to be an exact replica or use the original as an inspiration for the copyist's own talent; these will be dissimilar, but both are copies.

Reproductions are those articles made in imitation of an original pattern but on a commercial scale. Many people invest in reproduction furniture, feeling that the originals are too expensive or are unavailable. The paradox of this is that

164

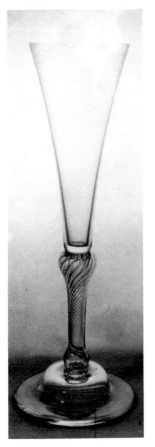

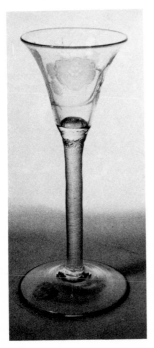

modern good quality, handmade reproduction furniture can be almost as expensive as the antique original. Such furniture is not made with intent to mislead. Most modern reproductions are marked with the maker's name. Recently a firm in America was reproducing the Burmese glass invented at the Mount Washington Glass Co. in the 1880's. It comes complete with an explanatory leaflet and is marked with its maker's name.

Fakes, on the other hand, are made with the express intention of being passed off as the originals, or rather to be sold at the prices which the originals will command. The examples of this kind of trickery are legion and hardly any class of goods which commands a high price has not been subject to this form of misrepresentation.

Having said all this, marks can be removed or altered, objects can appear in places which may lead one to suppose they are older than they are, and the unwary or unknowledgeable can let their enthusiasms get the better of them. It is these considerations which make it necessary to try and explain the pitfalls that beset the glass collector. For the sake of convenience I shall refer to them all as copies.

The copies I have come across fall into several well-defined groups:

a Nineteenth century copies having a good similarity to the originals.

b Nineteenth century copies based on eighteenth century styles but noticeably different in character.

c Later nineteenth and early twentieth century copies of early baluster styles.

d Modern copies of eighteenth century styles.

e Modern copies of nineteenth century styles.

I have already referred to *The Curiosities of Glassmaking* by Apsley Pellatt. This book, published in 1849, gave detailed descriptions of making the opaque twist rod from which the opaque twist stems were produced. At that time most glass was still being made by hand in the same manner that it had been made for centuries. It seems reasonable to assume, therefore, that there was nothing to prevent the glassmakers of the 1850's producing glasses identical to those of the 1750's. Bear in mind, though, that by the middle of the nineteenth century public taste had changed, and drinking glasses were then being made with larger bowls and more slender stems. Anyone producing styles a century out of date was obviously going against current practice. This consideration has led me to the conclusion that anyone copying an earlier style does it as an act of conscious effort. The glassmakers of 1750 were working in a tradition which was current, in which they had been raised through years of apprenticeship and which thus became an entirely instinctive and natural process. The glassmaker of 1850 setting out to achieve the same end had to refer to his model and think of what he was doing every step of the way. This inevitably produces a more contrived and self-conscious end result. It is possible, therefore, to detect a degree of regularity and a degree of stiffness in the good Victorian copy which the original lacks. As I said, this is not easy to convey in words but is an instinct acquired with experience.

As well as these very good copies of earlier glass, nineteenth century glassmakers produced opaque twist glasses with a twist which was in complete contrast to those I have just mentioned. They are composed of finer strands, more open in arrangement and generally with a much more gradual and irregular twist. They lack the substance and vigour of the earlier ones. These stems give themselves away when seen in conjunction with bowl sizes and shapes which are Victorian in character.

That leads me to the second group. These are glasses, usually engraved, which take their inspiration from eighteenth cen-

151 An oval cut glass bowl with the cutting typical of the late eighteenth century, but this was made in Bohemia/Czechoslovakia c. 1920.

166

152 A small Victorian sherry glass with Jacobite engraving. This is interesting since as the glass is so obviously of its period it would seem that the decoration was not added to deceive in any way. Perhaps there were Jacobite Societies as late as the 1880's.

tury originals but are expressed in a nineteenth century idiom. Among these are privateer glasses, Jacobite glasses and others bearing engraved commemorative sentiments. They differ from the originals in being larger and having coarser engraving. Eighteenth century privateer glasses are nearly all opaque twist glasses, about six inches high and with bucket bowls. The nineteenth century copy is about eight inches high with a bucket bowl which is wide in comparison to the height. The Jacobite glasses, while having the conventional emblems engraved on them (p. 121, illus. **104**) are up to 12 or 13 inches tall, a size of glass never made in the eighteenth century. I have recently seen a plain stemmed bucket bowl wine glass engraved with ships and 'Success to the British Fleet. 1759'. This compares to a glass in the Higgins Museum in Bedford engraved with the same sentiment, but the date 1749. In the eighteenth century, wheel engraved letters were generally produced by a series of straight strokes. The lettering on the former glass conforms to this method, but the date 1759 is carried out in the free-flowing continuous style of wheel engraving used for inscriptions in the late nineteenth century.

Other styles of the eighteenth century were copied, but given the proportions of the second half of the nineteenth century; bowls overpowering the stems and feet.

The third category produced some very good copies, and some flights of fancy. Before one has acquired the feeling for the style appropriate to any particular period it is not uncommon to encounter a glass which exhibits typical stylistic detail of a period, but in a combination which further experience would immediately make suspect. Two glasses which come to mind are a baluster stem glass with tall drawn trumpet bowl on a ball knop stem and folded foot. The other is a glass having a round funnel bowl on a multi-knopped stem, some of which contain air beads, the foot being domed and folded. The individual parts of these glasses are correct for period, but the combinations are wrong.

In contrast to these pseudo glasses, there are some very good copies which I am sure would mislead many people. These are harder to explain, but generally the clarity and brilliance of the metal is against them, and that sure give-away, a foot which is not quite true to period. Amongst these I have seen Silesian stemmed sweetmeats and baluster stemmed glasses. One firm which is known to have made these was Powell's Whitefriars Glassworks, where they copied glasses of many earlier periods. In the 1920's they even produced reconstructions of the glasses found as fragments on the Wealden glasshouse sites.

The next group of glass copies is probably the one which gives modern collectors the most trouble, if only because there are so many of them. These are copies of most of the eighteenth century styles and which were circulating freely some twenty years ago. No-one seems too sure where they originated, but I have heard both Italy and Norway suggested as their source.

Since they have many characteristics which proclaim their common origin and which can be compared to similar details of genuine glasses, I am sure that once these are appreciated the aspiring collector need not be caught out more than once.

1 They are invariably of soda metal (see page 39).

2 The metal of the bowl is usually slightly thicker than one would find in a genuine glass, and the bowl has a gathered, thickened rim which is much more irregular than one would expect in a genuine glass.

3 Twisted stems have three distinct characteristics.

   a Opaque twist stems are composed of threads of a greyish white colour in contrast to the dense opaque white of genuine ones, and on close inspection it will be seen that the texture of these threads is of a chalky, granular quality rather than the smooth surface of the true opaque twist.

   b Air twist stems have a close pattern of threads which give a congested and ravelled appearance instead of the well-defined and separated threads of earlier glasses. In addition, some of them contain air threads of a sharply rectangular appearance.

   c Mixed twist examples contain alternate strands of air and opaque enamel twisted into one pattern. I have not yet seen a genuine glass which did not have the two elements, air and enamel, clearly separated (see page 61).

4 Plain stem varieties, of which the drawn trumpet with air tear is most common, reveal themselves by the swelling at the base of the stem where it joins the foot. This is not like a base knop but more in the nature of a platform or step. This device became quite common in the later nineteenth century and is one of the significant details in Victorian glasses.

5 Some of them have plain feet which compare reasonably with original ones, but many have what appears to be a folded foot. On closer examination it may be seen that this is not a true fold, since there is not in fact a double layer of glass but a thickening of the rim with a step down which looks at first glance like a fold. The point to bear in mind here is that the fold was originally necessary to reinforce the thinness of the glass in the foot so that in an early glass the folded rim is still quite thin. In these later copies the 'folded' section at the rim will be twice as thick as in any genuine glass, the thickness of the remaining

part of the foot being at least as thick as in any plain footed glass of an earlier period.

6 While there is always the appearance of a pontil mark close examination will reveal that this is an impressed mark giving a roughened appearance to the metal. Most genuine glasses have a pontil mark showing a clean break.

Such is the varied nature of old hand-made glass that if any one of these points is taken in isolation (except 3c) I am sure that sooner or later an example will turn up which contradicts what I have said. However, when several of these failings appear together on one glass then I am sure that the glass will prove to be a copy. The following technique is a useful one for assessing any piece of glass. Do a mental balance sheet covering all the details and points one has learned to look for in old glass. If there are one or two points against and the rest in favour then the odds are that it is genuine; three or four points against and then it must be considered doubtful, to say the least.

The final group to consider are the modern copies of nineteenth century styles of both glass and decoration. These are being produced today both in this country and abroad. English-made copies include 'Bristol' blue glass and 'cranberry' glass. I have also seen modern copies of 'Mary Gregory' style decoration advertised recently. From abroad many imitations of the multi-coloured baskets and vases popular in Victorian times are being made in China, and the air-bubble filled lumps of pale green glass, generally called door dumps, are being made in Italy. All these are distinguishable by their strident colours and shiny surface finish and usually their lack of any wear marks, although these can be faked. The English makers of copies mark these articles with their name, but unfortunately these can be removed without too much difficulty. The best protection against being misled by these is to find the manufacturers' leaflets illustrating the patterns they make, and learn to recognise them. Finally, now that the interest in pressed glass is growing, I am beginning to find copies of the opaque glass commonly known as 'slag' glass. These are detectable by the shiny, oily appearance of the surface and the poor definition of the moulding. This leads me to believe that whoever is producing them is doing so by making a mould from an actual example, rather than from an original, or copy of, a metal mould. These copies carry the original factory marks and registration marks. These must surely come under the heading of fakes.

Chapter 9

About collecting

In years gone by collecting was usually the preserve of the wealthy intellectual, and many of our museums owe their finest exhibits, and sometimes their existence, to the scholarship of such people. Since the last war the picture has changed dramatically. The dissemination of knowledge, through books and television, about our domestic and cultural heritage has encouraged people to an appreciation of our past that has created a new generation of collectors which includes people from every walk of life.

Most collectable items carry distinguishing marks which help to make identification and attribution easy, but the glass collector is not so fortunate with his chosen subject as most other collectors. How then is one to get this experience? Little antique glass is marked, and the qualities and characteristics such as weight, colour and striation which the aspiring collector must familiarise himself with are just those qualities which do not lend themselves to illustration. So what opportunities are there for practical experience to supplement the textbooks? The problem is to find opportunities to handle a sufficient variety of glass objects that the appraisal of these factors become second nature.

It is my experience that there is a limited amount of old glass almost everywhere one looks, antique shops, stately homes, museums, but the places where one may find large quantities or fellow collectors are much fewer. It is important to find and visit these places, since there is much to be learned from the comparisons it is possible to draw when looking at a lot of glass assembled together, as well as from individual items. The two principal sources for large collections are museums and the auction rooms.

There are a number of museums with very good collections of glass which are permanently on display. Among these are:

The Victoria and Albert Museum   London
The Ashmolean Museum   Oxford

The Fitzwilliam Museum	Cambridge
The Higgins Museum	Bedford
The Pilkington Glass Museum	St. Helens, Lancashire
Broadfield House Glass Museum	Kingswinford, W. Midlands
The Huntley House Museum	Edinburgh
Mompesson House	Salisbury
The London Museum	Barbican, London
The City Art Gallery	Bristol
Laing Art Gallery	Newcastle-on-Tyne

These are by no means all the museums with collections of glass, but between them they cover the whole history of glassmaking in the British Isles. In addition to what is on display there are often reserve collections which are available to the serious student if reasonable and proper notice is given. Many smaller museums also have collections of glass which may not be on display, but are worth enquiring after. Remember that museums are not only repositories of the nation's heritage but are also there for the benefit of we, the public, and it is up to us to make use of them. Another service that museums offer is the identification and dating of objects which members of the public take to them. Bear in mind, though, that not every museum has experts in every subject. If you have something of specialist interest then it is better to approach a museum which, itself, has a specialist collection of that type of article.

The museum collections are static in that they don't readily dispose of their exhibits, so that a collection can be visited more than once and its contents used for reference purposes. Equally interesting, and more challenging, I think, are those auction houses which hold regular sales devoted entirely to glass. Sotheby's and Christie's are the principal ones, each holding four or five sales per year with from 200 to 300 items of glass in each sale. The glass in their sales is generally on display for several days beforehand, but one usually has to apply for a pass, in advance, to gain unrestricted access to view the contents. However, the porters in charge will usually hand over individual items for examination. The advantage of sales like this is that each one contains a wide variety of glass which changes with each sale. The catalogue provides useful descriptive material for the novice and, in due course, the list of prices realised, which one may order, acts as an indication of current prices. As a word of caution, don't read too much into prices realised unless you have viewed a sale, since condition and quality have a considerable bearing on price.

Most other sale rooms which feature glass regularly usually sell it in conjunction with their ceramics sales, and occasionally complete collections are offered at specialist sales in one or another of the provincial auction rooms. Sales where quantities of glass are offered usually attract all the specialist dealers and collectors, so prices are generally in line with current values. The best opportunities for buying bargains in sales are those where the glass is not well catalogued and the sale is not widely enough advertised to attract much attention. But that brings us back to the point of this chapter. How does one acquire the knowledge necessary to take advantage of these situations?

The other source of knowledge is that possessed by other collectors. Unfortunately, glass collecting being a somewhat specialist interest, there are never very many glass collectors in any particular area. Contact with other collectors can usually be made through local antique circles or societies, and for anyone who has reasonable access to London, The Glass Circle is a society which specialises in the study of glass of all periods and which draws its members from all over the country. It has published three books of its transactions which are all of interest to any serious student. They may be obtained from the publishers, Gresham Books, Old Woking, Surrey, GU22 9LH.

To sum up then. The best way to cultivate one's own judgement is to handle as much as possible. Don't be afraid to ask questions and be prepared to make mistakes. As long as it is not bought too dearly one should always learn something from one's excess of enthusiasm and write the cost off to experience. If there is one further point to be learned from this, it is that nobody has a monopoly of knowledge, and in the study of glassware particularly I am sure there is as much opportunity for the beginner as for the long time student to discover new information or come up with a fresh conclusion. By making the most of opportunities to handle glass, by discussing the subject with other people sharing the same interest and by reference to the wealth of published material one may eventually lay claim to that much overworked title of 'expert'.

With regard to the collection itself, I strongly recommend that a suitable glass fronted cabinet or display case be acquired. If it can be fitted with lights so much the better. Left exposed, glass quickly gathers dust and the more often it is handled to clean it the greater the risk of some mishap. Behind glass doors it may be seen to advantage, it is protected and will not become dirty so quickly. This applies equally to the modest collection of Victoriana as to a collection of rare, baluster stem glasses.

Glossary

Acid etching A pattern produced on glass by the action of acid, usually working through the gaps in an acid resistant film applied to the glass.

Air twist A pattern inside the stem of a glass produced by a series of elongated threads of air.

Annealing Relief of stresses in glass that have been caused by the blowing process. The glass is reheated to a little below melting point and allowed to cool slowly.

Composite stem A stem of a wine glass that comprises two or more different styles, such as air twist and plain stem or opaque twist and air twist.

Crizzling A fine crazing and cloudiness occasionally found in glass with incorrect proportions of raw ingredients. It is much associated with early Ravenscroft glass.

Cullet Broken glass formerly added to the glass pots to be remelted with the raw materials. There was once an active trade in cullet which explains why so few pieces of glass are found on glasshouse sites.

Facet stem A pattern of facets cut on to a plain stem from the late eighteenth century. Also known as a cut stem.

Flashed glass A thin layer of coloured glass laid over a thicker layer so that patterns of colour are produced when the outer layer is cut.

Flint glass Glass using calcined flint as a source of silica. In general, lead glass from the 1680's onward and any clear glass in the late nineteenth century.

Folded foot The rim of the foot of a drinking glass which has a double thickness to give extra strength. Most frequently seen up to 1750 but rare thereafter.

Gaffer The man in charge of a team of three or four glassmakers, and who does the blowing.

Gather The molten glass collected on the end of the blowing iron and from which the glass vessel is produced.

Incised twist A twisted spiral produced by a series of fine grooves on the outside of a drinking glass stem.

Knop A swelling on the stem of a drinking glass. Knops were most elaborate in the early eighteenth century; by the 1740's they were reduced to simple swellings in the stem.

Lead glass A type of glass developed by George Ravenscroft in the 1670's which contains a high proportion of lead oxide. Although common in the British Isles from that date onward, it was not generally adopted on the Continent until the late eighteenth century.

Merese A thin collar found between the bowl and stem of glasses, particularly rummers, c. 1800.

Metal A glassmaker's term for glass. It is probably explained by the similarity of molten glass and molten metal.

Moulding Shaping glass by pouring or blowing it into a mould.

Opaque twist A pattern of twisted opaque white or coloured threads of glass found on drinking glass stems. Also known as cotton or enamel twist.

Overlay A technique similar to that used for flashed glass, but the outer layer is thicker so that some relief-work can be obtained when the decoration is cut into it. Overlay was used in producing cameo glass.

Pontil The iron rod on which a glass object is supported after it has been removed from the blowing iron so that further work can be carried out on it. The mark left when the pontil has been removed is the pontil mark, which is characteristic of hand-made glass.

Pressed glass Glass made by a mechanised process of moulding that does not require a skilled glass-blower. Developed in the USA and widely used in the British Isles in the late nineteenth century.

Prunt A blob or button of glass applied to the outer surface of a glass vessel for decorative effect. It was often impressed with a pattern.

Rummer A large capacity short-stemmed drinking glass of the late eighteenth and the nineteenth centuries. The name may either be a corruption of the German word Roemer (a sixteenth century European drinking glass) or be derived from its use as a glass for rum-based toddy. Take your pick!

Seed A small particle of unmelted raw material or foreign matter found embedded in old glassware. One of the characteristics of old glass.

Soda glass Glass that does not contain lead. The standard type of glass before Ravenscroft.

Tear A bubble of air contained in the stem or in the base of the bowl of many eighteenth century glasses.

Trailing A fine thread of glass applied to the outside of a glass vessel for decorative effect. Its use dates back over 2000 years; in the nineteenth century a method of applying it mechanically was invented.

Wrythen A twisted pattern of ribs or lines incorporated in the body of a glass vessel.

Bibliography

There are many titles on the history of British glass, and each one offers some new knowledge or opinion which should stimulate the serious collector. Those I have listed, however, seem to me to offer the widest possible range of information for the least amount of reading.

To 1700

The Development of English Glassmaking 1560-1640, Eleanor S. Godfrey, Clarendon Press, 1975. A scholarly and readable account of the most formative years of the English glass industry. Well researched, and deserves to be more widely known.

The Glass Industry of the Weald, G. H. Kenyon, Leicester University Press, 1967. This covers all the work done by S. E. Winholt in his *Wealden Glass* of 1933 with further useful additions.

Ravenscroft to Victoria

Antique Drinking Glasses, A. Hartshorne, Brussel and Brussel, 1968. This is a reprint of *Old English Glasses,* first published in 1897. The first important book on glass from the collector's point of view. The text is dated but appendices giving original documents are most important.

Collecting Glass, Norman W. Webber, David and Charles. Good readable account of the subject.

English, Scottish and Irish Table Glass, G. Bernard Hughes, 1956. Contains a good number of illustrations showing glass depicted in paintings. Also has chapters dealing with minor articles of glassware like finger bowls, sweetmeats and candlesticks.

History of Old English Glass, Francis Buckley, 1925. Well researched, like all Buckley's books. Useful for original documents quoted. Good illustrations.

How to Identify English Drinking Glasses and Decanters 1680-1830, Douglas Ash, Bell, 1962. Still the best book describing the development of decanters.

An Illustrated Guide to 18th Century English Drinking Glasses, L. M. Bickerton, Barrie and Jenkins, 1971. Probably the widest range of illustrations of any book on English glass. Excellent reference work which also contains one of the very few comprehensive bibliographies on the subject. Already hard to obtain.

Old English Drinking Glasses, Grant R. Francis, Herbert Jenkins, 1926. Never reprinted, so it is hard to find and is expensive. Best for its illustrations, many of which appear nowhere else, and the section on Jacobite glass.

19th Century

English 19th Century Press Moulded Glass, C. Lattimore, Barrie and Jenkins, 1979. The first book to deal comprehensively with one of the most important aspects of Victorian glassmaking. Well researched and illustrated.

19th Century British Glass, H. Wakefield, Faber, 1961. A short text with good illustrations of, mainly, documented pieces.

Victorian Table Glass and Ornaments, Barbara Morris, Barrie and Jenkins, 1978. Most informative book yet on this wide subject.

Irish Glass

Irish Glass, D. Westropp, Herbert Jenkins, 1920. Recently re-published by Allen Figgis and Co., Dublin. A good account quoting many original documents.

Irish Glass, Phelps Warren, Faber, 1970. Covers the period 1780-1830. The best illustrations of a wide range of cut glass in any book yet.

General

Coloured Glass, Middlemas and Davis, Herbert Jenkins, 1968. Not to be confused with *Antique Coloured Glass,* which is currently in print. This is the only book aimed at this aspect of collecting.

Curiosities of Glass Making, Apsley Pellatt, David Boyne, 1849. Facsimile Reprint 1968 by The Ceramic Book Co., Newport. An excellent first-hand account of glassmaking by a working master craftsman.

A History of English and Irish Glass, 2 vols, W. A. Thorpe, Medici Society, 1929. Reprinted in one volume by Holland Press, 1969. I have included this book here because it is still the definitive work on the whole history of the subject from Roman times to the 20th Century. Rather academic in tone, but a must for the serious student. Has a tendency to date things earlier than current knowledge suggests.

An Illustrated Dictionary of Glass, H. Newman, Thames and Hudson, 1977. A useful reference work which updates Elville's *Dictionary* of 1961, but still has omissions.

Index